THE G.O.A.T: LeB

The Story of One of the Greate: time

By Kiril Valtchev

An Unauthorized Biography

DISCLAIMER

TABLE OF CONTENTS

INTRO

LeBron James is an American basketball player whose skills and talents were molded in the city of Akron, Ohio. He is currently one of the biggest sports icons in the world and is undoubtedly one of the best basketball players to ever play the game. LeBron played high school basketball at St. Vincent-St. Mary High School in his hometown of Akron, Ohio. The world quickly began to learn about *"The Kid from Akron".* LeBron averaged 18 points, and 6.2 rebounds a game just in his freshman year of high school. His high school team, The Fighting Irish, finished the year with a record of 27-0 and a division 3 state title. Scouts from major universities were all over him in no time. As high school progressed his stats and game continued to elevate beyond his peers. By the end of his senior year LeBron had become a high school basketball Phenom. Home games had to be moved to the University of Akron due to high ticket demands from fans, alumni, college and NBA scouts that wanted to watch him play. His athleticism was something you would see in video games. He also played wide receiver for St. Vincent- St. Mary's football team and was getting recruited by some of the nation's top division 1 programs. He was a simply a natural born athlete. At the end of his senior year, he had an important decision to make: go to college or straight to the NBA. Straight to the big leagues. LeBron remains the last high school basketball player to go straight to the NBA from high school. LeBron James began his basketball career as the number 1 draft pick from the Cleveland Cavaliers in 2003. The pressure to perform was set early on in LeBron's career due to the massive endorsements contracts and media frenzy he began to receive in high school. From his first NBA game, it was clear that LeBron was going to be a serious competitor. In his first NBA game depute, he scored 25 points against the Sacramento Kings. At the end of the season, LeBron was named NBA Rookie of the Year, finishing the season with 21 points, 5.5 rebounds and 5.9 assists per game. He had a maturity about the game that most players in the league lacked. Even though the Cavaliers failed to make the playoffs that year, LeBron continued to work hard on improving not only his game, but the overall dynamic of the team. He was a natural born leader.

LeBron earned his first NBA- All Star selection in 2005. His rise to superstar status was rivaled only by few. At the end of the 2004-2005 season, the Cavs still failed to make the playoffs, but their overall record improved drastically since LeBron joined the roster. At the end of the 2005-2006 season LeBron proved to be an absolute basketball machine, averaging 31.4 points, 7 rebounds and 6.6 assists per game. Those are superstar numbers. The pace at which he achieved those stats is godly. In the 2006-2007 season his stats slightly fell to 27.3 points, 6.7 rebounds, and 6 assists per game. Even though his stats took a slight decline LeBron was making the overall team better. All the other players on the team were becoming more efficient and dynamic players. That is how selfless LeBron was. He was distributing the ball more and shifting the whole team to become better, not only himself. The Cavs ended up making the playoffs in the 2005-06 season for the first time since 1998. They finished the season with a 50-32 record, second in the NBA Central division. The Cavs would go on to defeat the Washington Wizards in the first round of the playoffs, but were stopped in their journey in the second round of playoffs by the Detroit Pistons. LeBron took a team that had not been to the playoffs in almost a decade to the second round of playoffs in less than 3 years after entering the league. This wasn't luck, this was a champion and a basketball legend in the making. This is his story.

Chapter 1: Early life

LeBron James was born on December 30, 1984 in Akron, Ohio by 16-year-old single mother, Gloria Marie James. LeBron's father *(Anthony McClelland)* was in and out of jail majority of his life and was not around at all. Gloria raised LeBron all on her own. Growing up, life was a struggle for LeBron and his mom. Gloria bounced around retail and accounting jobs most of LeBron's life and finding steady work was often a challenge. They had to move frequently from apartment to apartment and got to know all the major neighborhoods of Akron. This was very hard for LeBron and his mother.

Despite her struggles, she continued to be a hard working and supportive mother and helped keep LeBron away from the violence of the streets. When LeBron was two years old she began dating Eddie Jackson who was frequently in and out of trouble. Even though Eddie was trouble, LeBron liked having a father figure around, but in the years that followed Eddie got sent to jail for drug trafficking and committing mortgage fraud. Gloria realized that LeBron would be in need of a more stable family environment and allowed him to move in with the family of Frank Walker, a youth football coach, who ended up introducing LeBron to the game of basketball at the age of nine.

From a very early age, LeBron had serious instincts for not only basketball, but all sports. LeBron played wide receiver in his pee wee football league where he scored 19 touchdowns in 6 games of his first year. Frank Walker became like a father figure to LeBron. Frank helped LeBron learn how to shoot and LeBron learned quickly. There was very little that was certain at this point in LeBron's life and future. The Walkers had three children of their own, and LeBron ended up sharing a room with Frankie Walker Jr., a football teammate who became one of his best friends. The Walkers were a working-class family and instilled hard work, perseverance, and dedication in LeBron. They made James wake up at 6:30 a.m. every day for school and made sure he finished his homework before basketball. Frank slowly taught LeBron how to shoot left handed layups and how to dribble. James picked up everything very quickly and his skills improved by the day. Walker could see LeBron's skills improving with every practice and he was quickly surpassing his peers. It was easy to see that there was something special about LeBron.

The Walkers enrolled LeBron in Portage Path Elementary, one of the oldest elementary schools in the city of Akron. His life slowly started shifting in a positive direction and LeBron was much happier. With a steady family dynamic around him, LeBron became more focused and was attending school every day. As the years progressed, LeBron played on an AAU team for the Northeast Ohio Shooting Stars. Alongside him were his friends Sian Cotton, Dru Joyce, and Willie McGee. The four of them became inseparable and called themselves the "Fab Four". They promised each other that they would attend the same high school and play basketball together. The four of them decided to attend St. Vincent-St. Mary High School.

Chapter 2: The High School Era

FRESHMAN YEAR

LeBron's quick rise to stardom begins with his freshman year in high school. There was a moment where even the king was nervous, scared and intimidated to play before a game. On the night of Dec.3 1999, at Cuyahoga Falls High School, LeBron was sitting on the bleachers by himself feeling nervous and worried about his first high school basketball game as a freshman. This would be his introduction to Northeast Ohio fans. James was intimidated because all the other players were bigger than him and had more confidence. Once the team got in the locker room before the game started, a guy named Maverick Carter stepped up and spoke to the team. At that time, Maverick was the only senior starter on the team. Once Maverick gave his speech to the team LeBron felt comfortable and ready to play. LeBron responds best to people that make him feel comfortable. Once LeBron started warming up for the game he had already forgotten about being nervous and was in the zone. The crowd slowly flooded the gym for the opening night and LeBron was ready to perform. The game started fast and the Irish took an early lead right from the tipoff. LeBron scored a few back to back breakaway layups and the crowd was going wild. LeBron was feeling confident to perform on the floor with the older players. The first half went quickly and the team was playing together and scoring effortlessly. By the end of the first half the Irish were up by 20 points. The rest of the game continued smoothly and the Irish ended up winning the game 76-40. James finished the game with 15 points and 8 rebounds, not bad for his first high school varsity game as a freshman.

The Irish ended up winning the next 26 games to have a perfect 27-0 record. They ended up winning the Division 3 state championship that season. LeBron finished the season with average of 18 points and 6.2 rebounds per game. What a way to start your high school basketball career, a perfect record, a state title and being the leading scorer on your team as a freshman. LeBron was on his way to becoming an Akron basketball legend.

>>>>> LeBrons freshman year game logs on the next page

LeBron's Freshman Season Game Logs (27-0)

Per game totals

Points: 18.0   **Steals:** 3.1
Rebounds: 6.2   **Blocks:** 1.0
Assists: 3.6   **Turnovers:** 2.1

Percentages

FG: 51.6
3FG: 31.6
FT: 79.7

Awards

All-Ohio Division III first team; Plain Dealer Best of the Best;
state tournament MVP.

DATE	OPPONENT	FG M-A	3FG M-A	FT M-A	PTS	REB	AS
Dec. 3	Cuyahoga Falls	6-10	1-2	2-2	15	8	2
Dec. 4	Cleveland Central Catholic	9-15	2-5	1-1	21	7	2
Dec. 7	Garfield	4-16	0-8	3-3	11	5	2
Dec. 17	Benedictine	10-16	2-4	5-6	27	4	1
Dec. 18	Detroit Redford (Mich.)	8-17	0-2	2-4	18	8	2
Dec. 28	Mansfield Temple Christian	9-16	0-1	2-2	20	6	1
Dec. 30	Mapleton	7-14	5-8	2-2	21	3	0
Jan. 4	Central-Hower	10-18	1-3	0-1	21	6	4
Jan. 7	Massillon	7-17	0-3	0-0	14	5	4
Jan. 11	Padua	5-12	1-2	3-3	14	4	8
Jan. 12	Maple Heights	4-12	0-5	0-0	8	8	5
Jan. 14	Linsly Academy (W.Va.)	7-12	0-0	3-3	17	1	5
Jan. 15	Western Reserve Academy	5-17	2-6	0-0	12	5	3
Jan. 25	Youngstown Ursuline	3-8	2-5	5-6	13	6	3
Jan. 28	Walsh Jesuit	6-17	0-2	3-4	15	6	2
Feb. 1	Coventry	9-15	2-4	2-2	22	6	4
Feb. 5	Ashland Crestview	10-12	2-3	1-2	23	2	5
Feb. 15	CVCA	7-17	1-3	2-3	17	6	4
Feb. 23	Youngstown Rayen	7-11	1-5	3-3	18	9	6
Feb. 27	Archbishop Hoban	11-17	3-6	2-3	27	7	4
PLAYOFFS							
Mar. 3	Loudonville	8-12	0-1	1-2	17	6	6
Mar. 6	Hillsdale	11-19	1-3	0-1	23	7	5
Mar. 11	Waynedale	7-15	0-2	3-4	17	11	4
Mar. 16	Newton Falls	6-11	0-1	2-2	14	6	2
Mar. 18	Villa Angela-St. Joseph	7-16	2-4	2-2	18	6	5
Mar. 24	Canal Winchester	6-12	0-3	7-9	19	11	2
Mar. 25	Jamestown Greeneview	10-12	2-4	3-4	25	9	5
Totals		199-386	30-95	59-74	487	168	96

SOPHOMORE YEAR

Before he even completed his sophomore year in high school, college scouts were already looking at LeBron. They quickly took notice of his talents and athletic abilities. Winning a state title and being the leading scorer on your team in your freshman year is no easy feat. In his sophomore year, LeBron averaged 25.2 points, 7.2 rebounds and 5.8 assists per game. This is a huge improvement over his freshman year and it helped solidify LeBron as a top tier competitor. His electrifying in game dunks slowly began in his sophomore year and LeBron had no trouble dunking on defenders who wouldn't get out of his way. He led the team to a 26-1 record along with yet another Division 3 state title for the second straight season. LeBron was simply unstoppable. That year he was named Ohio's *"Mr. Basketball"* of the year and was the first ever sophomore to do so. Not only was he named Ohio's *"Mr. Basketball"*, he also became the first sophomore player to be selected to the *USA Today All-USA First*

Team. These were accomplishments that were out of reach for so many players and LeBron earned them only as a sophomore. Along with having success on the court, LeBron was also excelling on the football field. He was also getting recruited on the football field and was named *First-Team All-State* as a wide receiver the same year. Imagine the feeling. LeBron was building his basketball resume and at the same time building a stellar football resume. That same year LeBron racked up 700 receiving yards and was simply dominating the competition.

>>>>> LeBrons sophomore year game logs on the next

LeBron's Sophomore Season Game Logs (26-1)

Per game totals
Points: 25.3   **Steals:** 3.7
Rebounds: 7.4   **Blocks:** 1.6
Assists: 5.5   **Turnovers:** 2.3

Percentages
FG: 58.4
3FG: 39.3
FT: 71.1

Awards
USA Today first-team; All-Ohio Division III first team; Mr. Bas-
ketball; Plain Dealer Player of the Year; state tournament
MVP; All-Ohio Division IV first team wide receiver in football.

DATE	OPPONENT	FG M-A	3FG M-A	FT M-A	PTS	REB	AS
Dec. 3	Cape Henry Collegiate (Va.)	8-12	3-5	4-10	23	4	2
Dec. 6	Garfield	12-19	2-5	8-11	34	6	5
Dec. 9	Orange	9-14	0-0	7-8	25	12	6
Dec. 16	Racine Case (Wis.)	12-20	4-6	1-1	29	5	8
Dec. 17	Detroit Redford (Mich.)	5-13	0-1	6-7	16	7	3
Dec. 19	Cleveland Central Catholic	8-19	1-4	4-6	21	6	9
Dec. 29	Ashland Crestview	7-12	0-3	1-1	15	3	9
Jan. 5	Massillon	10-18	1-3	3-5	24	7	9
Jan. 7	Kennedy Christian (Pa.)	7-13	2-5	4-8	20	9	4
Jan. 13	Oak Hill Academy (Va.)	13-26	5-11	2-4	33	4	4
Jan. 19	Youngstown Rayen	8-18	1-3	3-3	20	6	4
Jan. 25	Walsh Jesuit	13-20	0-2	5-8	31	7	4
Jan. 28	Buchtel	9-15	1-4	14-15	33	4	1
Feb. 2	Villa Angela-St. Joseph	4-9	1-2	6-10	15	7	10
Feb. 3	Benedictine	16-20	1-3	8-12	41	9	6
Feb. 10	Youngstown Ursuline	11-16	0-1	4-5	26	6	9
Feb. 11	Archbishop Hoban	11-17	2-3	3-3	27	2	7
Feb. 16	Western Reserve Academy	12-14	3-5	2-2	29	9	5
Feb. 21	George Jr. Republic (Pa.)	8-15	1-2	7-9	24	7	7
Feb. 25	Central-Hower	9-18	0-0	8-11	26	11	4
PLAYOFFS							
Mar. 3	United Local	9-15	0-3	1-2	19	9	5
Mar. 5	Lisbon David Anderson	13-19	1-3	4-5	31	6	7
Mar. 9	N. Middletown Springfield	6-14	1-2	1-4	14	7	6
Mar. 15	Hillsdale	10-26	1-4	3-4	24	14	6
Mar. 17	Villa Angela-St. Joseph	11-17	2-3	6-8	30	14	6
Mar. 22	Haviland Wayne Trace	12-19	0-1	5-6	29	9	0
Mar. 24	Casstown Miami East	11-14	0-0	3-5	25	10	3
Totals		**264-452**	**33-84**	**123-173**	**684**	**200**	**149**

JUNIOR YEAR

Following his successful sophomore season, all eyes were on what *"Mr. Basketball"* would do next. People wondered if the Irish could win another state title. The hype about LeBron was now at an all-time high. Scouts from every major university were at his games to watch him perform. Home games began to get moved to the University of Akron due to high ticket demands from fans, alumni, college and NBA scouts that wanted to watch him play. In his junior year James proved yet again that he was a serious contender. He averaged 28 points, 8.9 rebounds, 6 assists and 3 steals per game. His stats had improved to a level many high schools players dream of. He was named *Mr. Basketball* of Ohio, earned a spot on the All-USA First Team and was also named the 2001-2002 basketball Gatorade Player of the year. LeBron also appeared in SLAM Magazine that year which sparked his nationwide exposure and everyone wanted a piece of him.

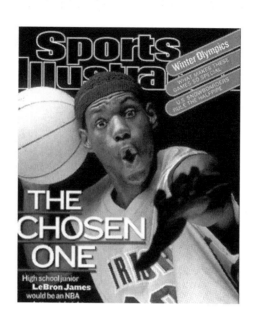

Despite LeBron's accomplishments during his junior year, the Irish failed to win another state title and ended up losing to Roger Bacon High School. LeBron felt like he was ready for the NBA and tried to declare for the draft after the season concluded. The problem was that he was still in high school and had another year to go. He tried to petition for an adjustment to the NBA's draft eligibility rules which required players to have finished high school. His petition was not successful which ended up bringing him even more widespread attention as he geared up for his senior year. In the offseason,

James continued to play AAU and appeared on the cover of Sports Illustrated and even ESPN Magazine. It was no question that his senior year was going to be a wild ride.

>>>>> LeBrons junior year game logs on the next page

LeBron's Junior Season Game Logs (23-4)

Per game totals

Points: 28.0 Steals: 3.0
Rebounds: 8.9 Blocks: 1.7
Assists: 6.0 Turnovers: 3.3

Percentages

FG: 56.5
3FG: 34.0
FT: 59.3

Awards

USA Today Player of the Year; All-Ohio Division II first
team; Mr. Basketball; Plain Dealer Player of the Year;
All-Ohio Division IV first team wide receiver in football.

DATE	OPPONENT	FG M-A	3FG M-A	FT M-A	PTS	REB	AS
Nov. 30	Avon Lake	13-19	2-3	0-1	28	12	6
Dec. 1	Germantown Acad. (Pa.)	15-23	2-3	6-14	38	17	4
Dec. 9	St. Louis Vashon (Mo.)	10-21	0-3	6-10	26	11	2
Dec. 15	Louisville Male (Ky.)	15-24	2-6	5-5	37	5	7
Dec. 22	Cincinnati Roger Bacon	9-18	0-4	11-20	29	9	4
Dec. 23	Detroit Redford (Mich.)	16-27	3-8	8-16	43	9	8
Dec. 28	St. Benedict (N.J.)	7-14	0-3	4-8	18	9	8
Dec. 30	*Amityville (N.Y.)*	*12-29*	*4-11*	*11-13*	*39*	*6*	*5*
Jan. 6	University School	9-15	1-2	1-3	20	7	1
Jan. 11	Franklin (Pa.)	10-15	1-2	1-2	22	3	6
Jan. 13	Brush	8-21	1-5	7-11	24	7	8
Jan. 18	East Liverpool	9-17	1-6	7-10	26	11	6
Jan. 20	Villa Angela-St. Joseph	10-15	3-6	0-3	23	8	11
Jan. 25	Walsh Jesuit	11-24	4-9	4-6	30	2	6
Jan. 27	Buchtel	13-22	4-10	3-5	33	8	10
Feb. 3	Archbishop Hoban	15-23	2-5	0-0	32	8	4
Feb. 10	*Oak Hill Academy (Va.)*	*12-28*	*2-8*	*10-13*	*36*	*10*	*5*
Feb. 17	*George Jr. Republic (Pa.)*	*8-20*	*0-5*	*4-6*	*20*	*10*	*1*
Feb. 20	Orange	15-24	0-4	3-5	33	7	8
Feb. 24	Central-Hower	11-18	1-2	1-4	24	14	3
PLAYOFFS							
Mar. 1	Firelands	10-13	1-1	1-3	22	8	5
Mar. 6	Archbishop Hoban	7-10	4-6	2-3	20	4	6
Mar. 9	Central-Hower	13-23	1-7	5-8	32	17	8
Mar. 13	Warrensville Heights	6-12	1-2	3-4	16	10	8
Mar. 16	Ottawa-Glandorf	8-12	1-3	4-6	21	16	9
Mar. 21	Poland Seminary	14-22	4-10	0-1	32	9	6
Mar. 23	*Cincinnati Roger Bacon*	*14-22*	*3-7*	*1-2*	*32*	*4*	*6*
Totals		**300-531**	**48-141**	**108-182**	**756**	**241**	**161**

SENIOR YEAR

In his senior year, LeBron averaged 30.4 points, 9.7 rebounds, 4.9 assists and 2.9 steals per game. His talent and skills were obvious to anyone who watched him play. Everyone's question seemed to be, what would happen next? LeBron's senior year was full of pressure and widespread controversy that he didn't expect. It started off shaky with his mother Gloria creating problems when a bank used LeBron's future earning potential to approve them for an $80,000 loan to purchase a Hummer H2 for LeBron's 18th birthday. This sparked tons of publicity and prompted an investigation by the OHSAA (Ohio High School Athletic Association). People began to talk and LeBron's reputation and his last high school season were now in jeopardy. OHSAA guidelines state that no amateur may accept any gift valued over $100 as a reward for athletic performance. Later on during the season, LeBron accepted two throwback jerseys of Wes Unseld and Gale Sayers which were valued at over $900 from the company NEXT, an urban clothing store supplier, in exchange to have his pictures displayed in their stores. Once the OHSAA found out about the exchange they stripped him of his eligibility to play. This was a huge disappointment to the rest of his team and would make it very difficult for the Irish to win another state title without James on the roster. LeBron was determined to make a comeback and ended up appealing the ruling. The judge that was responsible for the case blocked the ruling and reduced the penalty to a two-game suspension and allowed LeBron to play the remainder of the season. As a result of LeBron's ruling the team was forced to forfeit one of their wins, which ended up being their only loss for the season.

After the ruling, LeBron had one focus and one focus only. He wanted to bring home that state championship. Despite the turbulent year that LeBron had, the Irish managed to secure a third state championship title. As a result of the win, James was selected to be on the *All-USA First Team* for a third straight time and was selected as *Mr. Basketball* of Ohio yet again. He also went on to win the MVP award at the McDonald's All-American game. He did however lose his NCAA eligibility because he ended up participating in more than two high school-all-star events which is prohibited by NCAA rules. However, James didn't have his sights set on playing college ball. He didn't want to wait. He had his sights on much bigger things. James declared that he was going to enter the NBA draft and skip college ball. The future of basketball would never be the same.

>>>>> *LeBrons senior year game logs on the next page*

LeBron's Senior Season Game Logs (25-1)

Per game totals
Points: 30.4   Steals: 2.9
Rebounds: 9.7   Blocks: 1.9
Assists: 4.9   Turnovers: 2.8

Percentages
FG: 56.0
3FG: 38.2
FT: 67.8

Awards
All-Ohio Division II first team; Mr. Basketball; Plain Dealer
Player of the Year; state tournament MVP.

DATE	OPPONENT	FG M-A	3FG M-A	FT M-A	PTS	REB	AS
Nov. 30	*Wellston	4-9	2-6	1-2	11	4	2
Dec. 1	George Jr. Republic (Pa.)	9-18	1-5	2-2	21	14	7
Dec. 7	Chicago Julian (Ill.)	5-17	1-5	4-5	15	16	6
Dec. 12	Oak Hill Academy (Va.)	12-25	2-6	5-8	31	13	6
Dec. 15	New Castle (Pa.)	14-22	2-5	2-4	32	10	4
Dec. 17	Willard	15-24	6-9	0-0	36	8	2
Dec. 22	Strawberry Mansion (Pa.)	7-17	3-9	9-11	26	7	7
Dec. 28	Columbus Brookhaven	11-22	1-6	4-7	27	10	3
Jan. 4	Mater Dei (Calif.)	8-24	0-9	5-5	21	9	7
Jan. 7	Villa Angela-St. Joseph	16-27	2-7	6-7	40	8	3
Jan. 12	Detroit Redford (Mich.)	12-20	2-4	4-5	30	14	4
Jan. 14	Mentor	19-25	11-17	1-2	50	9	2
Jan. 20	R.J. Reynolds (N.C.)	14-23	1-5	3-6	32	10	2
Jan. 24	Walsh Jesuit	10-17	2-6	8-8	30	5	8
Jan. 26	*Buchtel*	*11-21*	*0-6*	*3-3*	*25*	*15*	*8*
Feb. 2	Canton McKinley	Ruled ineligible to play					
Feb. 8	L.A. Westchester (Calif.)	21-34	6-9	4-8	52	7	2
Feb. 14	Zanesville	19-26	4-7	4-5	46	4	5
Feb. 16	Kettering Alter	10-17	0-3	2-3	22	11	3
Feb. 24	Firestone	Ruled ineligible to play					

PLAYOFFS

DATE	OPPONENT	FG M-A	3FG M-A	FT M-A	PTS	REB	AS
Feb. 28	Kenmore	13-23	4-5	0-2	30	2	6
Mar. 4	Archbishop Hoban	11-17	1-3	1-3	24	6	3
Mar. 8	Central-Hower	17-30	4-8	3-3	41	14	5
Mar. 13	Tallmadge	8-13	3-5	0-0	19	6	9
Mar. 15	Ottawa-Glandorf	11-19	0-3	3-7	25	11	5
Mar. 21	Canton South	8-16	1-6	2-4	19	9	6
Mar. 22	Kettering Alter	10-21	1-3	4-8	25	11	2
Totals		**295-527**	**60-157**	**80-118**	**730**	**233**	**117**

Chapter 3: Forget College, Straight to the League

NBA DRAFT

With the first pick in the 2003 NBA draft the Cleveland Cavaliers select LeBron James. Cleveland fans would never forget those words. There was much speculation whether or not LeBron would be the first pick in the NBA draft. LeBron was happy to stay home and play for his hometown team. His main focus would be to turn the Cleveland franchise around and take them to the NBA finals. It would be the start of an era that would ignite the Quicken Loans arena for decades to come.

The endorsements, fans and critics came pouring in his first season with the Cavs. In his very first game against the Sacramento Kings, LeBron scored 25 points and set a NBA record for the most points scored by debut player. He was absolutely explosive in his first game. The crowd loved to watch him because he played the game with a tenacity and desire to win. LeBron went on to average 20.9 points, 5.5 rebounds, and 5.9 assists per game in his first season with the Cavaliers. He had a season high of 41 points on 3/27/2004 against the New Jersey Nets and it showed everyone that the kid from Akron was here to stay and make his mark on the game. It was no question that LeBron had talent, but would he be able to turn the Cavaliers around? The Cavs ended the season with a record of 35-47 and failed to make the playoffs. Even though they failed to make the playoffs, with LeBron on the roster, they had a massive 18 game improvement from the previous year. It became apparent that he was there to improve the dynamic of the team and push everyone around him to perform better.

ROOKIE OF THE YEAR

At the end of the regular season, LeBron was name NBA Rookie of the Year. The other contenders for the Rookie of The Year Award during 2004 included:

- Carmelo Anthony (Denver Nuggets)
- Dwayne Wade (Miami Heat)
- Kirk Hinrich (Chicago Bulls)
- Chris Bosh (Toronto Raptors)
- Udonis Haslem (Miami Heat)
- Marquis Daniels (Dallas Mavericks)
- T.J. Ford, (Milwaukee Bucks)

- Leandro Barbosa (Phoenix Suns)

- Josh Howard (Dallas Mavericks)

LeBron surely had some great competition during his first NBA season and many of those players competed on a collegiate level prior to entering the NBA. However, LeBron was a different player all around. He wanted to build a team dynamic that would have a central focus towards bringing home a championship to Cleveland. This would not be an easy task to accomplish and it would require the team to work hard together every day in order to improve to the level required to win a championship.

Chapter 4: The Beginning

2004-2005 Season

The new and improved Cleveland Cavaliers had everyone wondering, could the kid from Akron really turn around one of the worst teams in the NBA? The Cleveland Cavaliers began their first 20 games of LeBron's second season with a 12-8 record. This was a massive improvement over their previous season. LeBron had set the tone and it was clear that he was there to turn the team around. The next 20 games the Cavaliers managed to maintain their winning percentage and held a record of 24-16. They were far from being a power NBA team, but fans and critics were shocked at how quickly the team was rebuilding and improving. LeBron's talent and leadership was obvious on the court, as he went on to average 25 points, 7.4 assists and 7.4 rebounds per game. He was still only 19- years-old at that time. The city of Cleveland was witnessing the birth of the King.

Heading into the middle of the season, LeBron was voted to be a starter on the *Eastern Conference All-Star Team*. Becoming an All-Star starter in just his second season in the NBA, LeBron quickly established himself as one of the top players in the league. LeBron scored 13 points, 6 assists and 8 rebounds in a win against the West. As LeBron's rise to stardom continued that season, the Cavs winning season slowed down. They played a decent season, but still needed to improve if they planned on winning a championship. They finished the season with a 42-40 record and failed to make the 2005 NBA playoffs. Despite having a winning season, the Cavs decided to fire their head coach Paul Silas with roughly 20 games left in the regular season for not helping the team stay on the winning streak they started the season off with. They replaced him with head coach Brendan Malone and the plan was for him to help boost the team's record so they could make the playoffs. Even though the plan didn't work, their improvement over the previous seasons record of 35-47 was a testament to the impact James was having on the team.

2005-2006 Season

LeBron had done a great job improving his stats and the team's record the previous season, but would he manage to improve enough so the team could make the playoffs? Getting the Cavs to the playoffs this season would become LeBron's central focus. He wanted to live up to his reputation and catapult his team to success.

Heading into the new season the Cavaliers ended up hiring Mike Brown as their head coach. His focus would be on helping to shift the Cavaliers into a top defensive team. The Cavaliers also decided to pick up Larry Hughes, a dynamic point guard who was averaging 15 points per game and was in his prime. They believed Hughes's versatility along with LeBron's explosiveness would pair off well for the team. With a new and much improved management and roster, things began to look up for the Cavs.

Even though things were looking great for the Cavs, they started off at the same pace as the previous season with a 31-21 record heading into the All-Star weekend. This was pretty much where they stood the previous season, but LeBron's game and stats were elevating to superstar levels. Going into the All-Star weekend, LeBron was averaging 31.2 points, 6.6 assists and nearly 7 rebounds a game. With those kind of stats it was no question that he would get voted in as an All-Star starter. The *2006 NBA All-Star Game* was played on Sunday, February 19th at the Toyota Center in Houston, Texas. LeBron had a monster night. The East was down by 21 points at the half, but LeBron's hot shooting helped the East turn the game around. The score was tied with 16 seconds remaining in the fourth quarter. Dwayne Wade, who dropped 20 points, hit the game winning layup to help the East seal a victory. LeBron dropped 29 points along with 6 rebounds. His performance helped push the East to a two point win over the West. It was an extremely close game in the fourth quarter which had over 10 different lead changes and an ending score of 122-120. As a result of the win, LeBron was awarded with his very first *All-Star MVP* award. He would go down in history as the youngest player to receive an **NBA All-Star MVP** award at the age of 21. Needless to say, LeBron had one successful weekend.

After the All-Star weekend, it was time to get back to reality and put the focus on improving the Cavs record so they could have a chance of making the playoffs. The Cavs were very conscious of how their previous season took a downturn after the All-Star weekend and were determined not to make the same mistake twice. Their focus still seemed off and the Cavs went on to lose five straight games after the All-Star weekend. It was time for LeBron to really showcase his talents, pull the team out of the gutter and back on the road to success. With LeBron's leadership the Cavs went on a 9-game winning streak and put themselves back on the playoff map.

At the end of the season the Cavs had ended a seven-year steak. They had finally made the playoffs. They ended up finishing the season with a 52-30 record. LeBron was awarded **All-NBA First Team Honors** for the first time in his career. He was also one of the youngest players to ever receive the award.

James had accomplished a goal that seemed unreachable to critics, fans and even some of the Cavs owners. He had taken a failing NBA franchise and managed to bring them to the playoffs within 3 years of entering the league. He was creating a basketball resume that would rival the likes of Kobe Bryant and Michael Jordan. This was not just a basketball star, he was a hometown hero and a legend in the making.

In the first round of playoffs the Cavs went on to face the Washington Wizards. In the regular season the Wizards had beaten the Cavs 3-1. They were a very dominant team offensively and the Cavs would have to seriously step up their defense if they planned on advancing past them in the playoffs. The Wizards had a stacked roster. They had one of the deadliest shooters in the league on their team, Gilbert Arenas. He was in the midst of his prime and proved to be a tough opponent. They also had Antawn Jamison, a 6'8 power forward who was averaging 20 points per game and had not missed a single game that season. Another prominent player that the Wizards had at that time was Caron Butler, a 6'7 small forward who was averaging 17 points a game and was solid defensive player. In the first round playoff game, LeBron was absolutely unstoppable. He put up 32 points, 11 rebounds and 11 assists. A triple double, not a bad way to start off your first playoff appearance. It was a testament to his dedication towards making the Cavs a championship team. The rest of their games against the Wizards were tough, but LeBron's leadership pushed the team to victory. He averaged 35 points, 5.7 assists and 7.5 rebounds during his first round of playoffs. He proved to fans and critics that he could perform when the pressure was on. The Cavs ended up winning the series and prepared to face their next opponent, the Detroit Pistons. The Detroit Pistons were Eastern Conference Champions the previous season and the Cavs knew how serious of an opponent they would be. They had the best record in the Eastern Conference that season with 64 wins and 18 losses. The stakes were high and the pressure to perform was even higher.

The Pistons were very hungry for another run at the title as they had lost in the finals the previous season to the San Antonio Spurs. Neither team would go down without a fight. The Pistons had a veteran team of players consisting of Ben Wallace, Rip Hamilton, Rasheed Wallace, Tayshaun Prince and Chauncey Billups. They were no strangers to the playoffs or to winning championships. They had won an NBA title in 2004 and were hungry for more. The first two games were won quickly by the Pistons and people began to wonder if this would end up being a four-game sweep. The next two games the Pistons got a little too comfortable on the defensive end and the Cavs evened up the series at 2-2. The Cavs went on to win the next game and the doubt about their ability to perform against the Pistons quickly vanished. The next game was extremely close, but the Pistons managed to win 84-82. The series were now tied at 3-3 and it was off to the Palace of Auburn Hills in Michigan for Game 7.

Game 7 started of extremely well for James, as he went on to score 10 of his 15-field goal attempts during the first half of the game. Unfortunately, he ended up missing his first seven shots of the second half, scoring just 1 out of 9 in the third and fourth quarter combined. This gave the Pistons a healthy lead over the Cavs and they ended up winning the game 79-61. LeBron averaged 26 points, 8.6 rebounds and 6 assists in the 7 game series. The Pistons defense was simply too much for the Cavs in Game 7. Despite their loss, the Cavs had an epic season and James continued to improve on all levels of his game. Having almost beaten the previous Eastern Conference Champions, it was evident that the Cavs and James were evolving. In the off season, James was determined to improve his craft and make another run at the title. The future for LeBron and the Cavs was looking bright.

2006-2007 Season

This season LeBron proved to fans that he was one of the best players in the league. The Cavs ended the regular season with a 50-32 record like they had the previous year. They now had their sights set on getting to the NBA finals. LeBron averaged 27.3 points, 6.7 rebounds, and 6 assists per game. With every season LeBron had shown major improvements in his game and managed to elevate the team to new heights.

The Cavs were back in the playoffs and were determined to get to the finals. They began the playoffs much like they did the previous year. They faced the Washington Wizards in their first round which sparked the beginning a competitive rivalry. Going into the playoffs this year, the Cavs played as a cohesive unit and managed to sweep the Wizards in 4 games. The team was focused, ready and hungry for a shot at the title.

In their second round of the playoffs the Cavs Went on to face the New Jersey Nets. The Nets were a stacked team with veteran players who were no strangers to the playoffs. The Nets featured All-Star players Richard Jefferson, Jason Kidd and the half-man, half-amazing, Vince Carter. It was no question that this round of playoffs would be full of high caliber competition and highlights that would be shown on ESPN for years to come. The series started off very tight and each game managed to stay extremely close. Even though the games stayed close, the Cavs beat the Nets in 6 games. LeBron and the Cavs were headed to the Eastern Conference Finals to face an opponent they were very familiar with, the Detroit Pistons. Going into the finals, the Pistons were considered a better team than the Cavs. Even though the matchup round was different, the series started in the same way as last year. Detroit took full advantage of the first two home games and won them both. The first game was a very frustrating start for James, scoring a career playoff low of just 10 points. It was no question that the Detroit Pistons were a strong defensive team. The Cavs were more than aware that they were in the same predicament as the previous year and knew that they had to step their game up if they wanted a shot at the title. The criticism was coming from all angles about LeBron and the Cavs. James would however recover in Games 3 and 4 to carry the Cavs to a win. In Game 3 James put up 32 points, 9 rebounds and 9 assists to lead the Cavs to an 88-82 win over the Pistons. The next game LeBron dropped 25 points, 11 assists and 7 boards to secure a 91-87 win for the Cavs. The series were tied up again at 2-2. In Game 5, LeBron proved to fans and critics why he was the King. The game was extremely close through each quarter and there were over 10 lead changes in the second half of the game. The Cavs ended up winning the game 109-107, in an intense double overtime battle at the Palace of Auburn Hills. LeBron's performance was nothing short of legendary. Halfway into the 4th quarter LeBron had 19 points and the Cavs were up 79-78. LeBron began a scoring streak that baffled everyone who watched. In a post-game interview following the Pistons loss, point guard Chauncey Billups was asked about LeBron's performance. He simply responded with the following.

"We threw everything that we had at him, we just couldn't stop him". In less than 16 minutes of game time, LeBron went on to score 29 of the Cav's 30 points, and the team's final 25 points on 11-of-13 shooting from the field. He forced the game into overtime with an electrifying dunk with only 9 seconds remaining in the game. The game ended up going into a second overtime. LeBron carried the team to a win by driving down the lane and scoring a layup with only 2 seconds remaining. It was a playoff performance that would go down in the books as legendary. LeBron finished the night with 48 points, 9 rebounds and 7 assists. The Cavs now led the Pistons 3-2 and were only one game away from becoming the Eastern Conference Finals Champs. James was making NBA history and becoming one of the most talked about athletes in the world. The Cavs ended up crushing the Pistons in game 6 with a final score of 98-82. LeBron finished the game with 20 points, 14 rebounds and 8 assists. The Cavs had done it. They were headed to the NBA finals to face the San Antonio Spurs.

The San Antonio Spurs were a seasoned and

disciplined team who was notorious for winning NBA championships. Heading into the finals the Spurs were heavily favored to win. They were much more experienced and knew what they had to do in order to win. Their main goal was to shut down LeBron defensively. This was definitely easier said than done. They knew if they could contain LeBron's scoring they would be able to dictate the flow of the game. The Spurs managed to start the finals off strong by winning the first game 85-76. They held LeBron to 14 points and forced him to take tough shots from the field which he could not connect on. LeBron had a terrible shooting night making 4 out of 16 shots he attempted. The Spurs discipline and experience was working out well.

The next two games the Spurs continued to dominate and pulled away with a 3-0 lead over the Cavs. James got a taste of what elite NBA finals competition looked like. Even though LeBron showed glimpses of brilliance, the Spurs were prepared and knew how to respond to everything he brought their way. The strong leadership and experience of Tim Duncan, Tony Parker, Manu Ginobili and Bruce Bowen would prove to be too much for LeBron and the Cavs. The Spurs ended up beating the Cavs in a 4-game sweep and became the 2007 NBA Champions. LeBron continued to train in the off-season and prepared to make another run at the championship the following season. Even though the Cavs lost, it proved that they were a high caliber team who was capable of winning a championship.

2007-2008 Season

It was no question that the Cavs could use some improvements in their lineup in order to give them a winning edge. They needed a strong defensive adjustment in their lineup if they planned to beat a team like the Spurs in the finals. To much surprise, they stuck with their current lineup of LeBron, Ilgauskas, Gooden, Pavlovic and Hughes.

In the 2007 - 2008 season, strong teams began to form in the Western Conference and the Cavs needed to adjust if they wanted to remain competitive. It was the year that the Boston Celtics brought together Kevin Garnett, Paul Pierce and Ray Allen. They would get coined as the *"Big 3"*. It was clear that the Cavs were not improving this season and it prompted a mid-season trade to help shift their performance on track. They ended up trading Larry Hughes and Drew Gooden for Delonte West and Ben Wallace. They also went on to add shooting guard Wally Szczerbiak who ended up being a good addition to the Cavs.

With the new additions to their roster, the Cavs had a tough time adjusting and ended the regular season with a only 45-37 record. They had won 5 games less than the previous season and the critics began to talk. LeBron had a successful season averaging 30 points, 7.9 rebounds and 7.2 assists per game. Would that be enough to take the Cavs to the finals? The big 3 in Boston had an amazing season with a 66-16 record. It was the best record in the league that season and it let everyone know that the Celtics had their sights set on winning an NBA title.

The Cavs began their first round of playoffs just like the past two. They faced the Washington Wizards. The rivalry was different this year as some players on the Wizards began saying that LeBron was an overrated player. LeBron was no stranger to the skeptics and answered strong by scoring 32 points to lead the Cavs to a win in Game 1. The series went to Game 6 in which the Cavs proved to be the better team with 105-88 victory over the Wizards. The Celtics were a very dominant team and were in the middle of an intense seven game series against the Atlanta Hawks. The Cavs knew that if the Celtics lost against the Hawks they would be at a huge advantage to win the Eastern Conference Finals again. The Celtics ended up beating the Hawks in Game 7. It was no question that it was going to be nothing short of a dogfight to advance to the finals. Even though the Cavs were average in the regular season, they were playing very well in their first round of playoffs. Would they be able to play good enough to take out the Celtics?

The first two games were played at TD Garden in Boston and the Celtics did not waste a chance to use their home court advantage. The series quickly turned in Celtics favor as they won the first 2 games with ease. They shut James down in Game 1 and rest of the team had trouble adjusting. Game 3 was played at home and the Cavs were finally able to turn things around and win the game 108-84. The Cavs also ended up winning the next game at home 88-77. The series were now tied 2-2 and it was back at the Garden for Game 5. The Celtics were a very scrappy team at home. Each quarter was extremely close with less than a 5-point deficit throughout the whole game. LeBron played an incredible game and finished with 35 points, 3 rebounds and 5 assists. Unfortunately, his performance in Game 5 wasn't enough to win the game and the Celtics ran away with 96-89 victory. Game 6 was another extremely close game which the Cavs ended up winning 74-69. LeBron had 32 points, 12 rebounds and 6 assists. Game 7 was going to be played at the Garden. There was

a ton of pressure on LeBron and the Cavs to perform. LeBron scored 45 points in Game 7, but it wasn't enough to take down the Celtics. The Celtics ended up winning the game with a 97-92 victory. The Celtics would go on to beat the Los Angeles Lakers that year and win the NBA title. LeBron and the rest of the Cavs had some serious thinking to do in the off-season. Would they continue on their quest to secure an NBA title or would they crumble and split up?

The Summer Olympics

In the summer, LeBron went on to compete in the *2008 Beijing Summer Olympics*. The USA had once been a dominant force in the Olympics and were in the process of getting back to the level they once were at. Their 2008 starting five featured Dwight Howard, Chris Paul, Kobe Bryant, Dwyane Wade and of course LeBron James.

With a lineup of that stature, the team stood confident in their abilities to perform. They were ready to showcase their talents to the rest of the world and prove that the US was a dominant force in the game of basketball.

LeBron went on to average 15.5 points, 3.8 assists, and 5.2 rebounds in the Summer Olympics. He got to experience and play against a wide variety of skilled players which would go on to improve his overall game. The US went on to become gold medalists, by beating Spain in a very close game. James got to see how superstars like Kobe Bryant, Dwyane Wade performed and responded in tough game situations. The Olympics were a tremendous success and learning experience for LeBron. He would use his experience in the Olympics to further elevate his own game.

2008 - 2009 Season

After having played with a superstar lineup in the Summer Olympics, LeBron was ready to continue improving his game and elevate his team to new heights. The Cavs struggled to identify a core lineup the previous season with the addition of Ben Wallace and Delonte West. Their main problem was that they didn't have a true point guard that could control the flow of the game. They had a mixture of guards who they constantly rotated, but not a true point guard. They had Daniel Gibson, Damon Jones, and Delonte West. None of them were true point guards that could lead the team. To create a more controlled and synchronized team, the Cavs brought on Maurice Williams. He was a 6'1, 198 lbs. point guard who would be an excellent addition to the team. He had previously played 4 seasons with the Milwaukee Bucks and was in the midst of his prime.

Following the Cav's loss to the Celtics, they were determined to get another run at the title. The Cavs went on to have a record breaking year with a new franchise record. They best record in the Eastern Conference that season with 66 wins and 16 losses. That season LeBron averaged 28.4 points, 7.6 rebounds and 7.2 assists per game. Also, for the first time in his career, LeBron become league MVP that season. This was a testament to his will and dedication to not only his game, but also his team.

The Cavaliers began their playoff series strong by sweeping the Detroit Pistons and the Atlanta Hawks. After the Cavs beat the Pistons and the Hawks they had some time to rest and wait for the battle that was going between the Orlando Magic and the Celtics to be over. The two teams were very well matched against each other and the series ended up going to 7 games. At the end of it all the Orlando Magic came out victorious and beat the Celtics.

In the regular season the Magic had beaten the Cavs 2-1. There were obvious mismatch issues for Cleveland. They knew they would have to make adjustments in their lineup to keep up with the fast- pace gameplay of the Magic. The Magic had dominant center Dwight Howard, one of the best 3 point shooters Rashard Lewis and a solid point guard Jameer Nelson. They also had young rising star J.J Redick and another sharpshooter Hedo Turkoglu. They were a well-balanced team and played very disciplined basketball. The Magic had proven they could shoot outside the arc and dominate in the paint, but could they stop LeBron?

Going into the first game many people thought that the Cavs were at a huge advantage because they were well rested, while the Magic only had a few days rest. Even though LeBron could adjust to the fast tempo play of the Magic, the rest of his team was falling behind. The Magic were extremely efficient and could distribute the ball quickly to take high percentage shots. The 1st half couldn't have gone better for the Cavs. They were distributing the ball well and wearing Orlando's defense down. At halftime, the Cavs were up 63-48 and looked like a team that was ready for the NBA finals. In the second half of the game things began to turn the other way in favor of the Magic. They quickly picked up the tempo in the 2nd half and began to score relentlessly. Their offense was flowing and Rashard Lewis was draining 3's left and right. In the last minute of the 4th quarter Rashard Lewis drained a deep 3-pointer that put the Magic up by one point. The Cavs were not able to answer back. LeBron had a monster Game 1 dropping 49 points, 6 rebounds and 8 assists. Unfortunately, LeBron's performance would not be enough to get a win and the Magic went on to win the game 107-106. It was clear that this series was going to be a battle.

Game 2 started very much like Game 1. The Cavs had a 23-point lead in the game at one point and were determined not to have a repeat of Game 1. The Magic somehow ended up finding a way to come back from the 23-point deficit and tie the game by the fourth quarter with 30 seconds to go. LeBron drove down the lane with 30 to go and accidentally took 1 extra step and was called for a travel. On the next possession down the court, Hedo Turkoglu scored a jumper to put the

Magic up 2 points at 95-93 with only 1.3 seconds left in regulation. The Cavs had a very small chance of winning, but that's all LeBron needed. The Cavs inbounded the ball to LeBron at the top of the key and he hit a 3 point dagger to win the game at the buzzer. The crowd went absolutely wild and the rest of the Cavs team rushed on the court to celebrate the win. It was an epic shot that was replayed over and over on ESPN.

As great as LeBron's game winning shot was, the Cavs had to rethink their game plan. They couldn't allow themselves to continue letting the Magic come back from such huge deficits and expect to win the series. The first two games were at home for the Cavs and they needed to seriously step up if they planned to win the next 2 roads games.

In Game 3 the Magic ended up wearing down the Cavs defensively and won 99-89. They didn't waste the opportunity to take home court advantage. Despite LeBron's 41-point performance in Game 3 it wasn't enough to bolster a win. Game 4 ended up being another very close game which the Magic won 116-114.

LeBron's 44-point performance in Game 4 wasn't enough to get a win. He needed the rest of his team to step up and help. The series were now 3-1 and many people started to believe that it was over for the Cavs. The Cavs needed a miracle to win.

Game 5 would end up being the miracle the Cavs were looking for. LeBron was a relentless force in Game 5 and would do anything to win. He put up a triple double that night which consisted of 37 points, 14 rebound and 12 assists. LeBron led his team to a 112-102 win over the Magic. The Cavs won the game by forcing the Magic to 12 turnovers and limiting the whole team to only 12 assists. It became clear to the Cavs that if they wanted to win they needed to shut down the Magic on the defensive end. Game 6 was back to Orlando and the Cavs had to win or they would be out of the playoffs.

In Game 6 the Magic went back to their core game, distributing the ball inside and out and draining 3's. They picked up the flow of their tempo in Game 6 and began to wear down the Cavs. They ended up shooting 12-29 from behind the arc and only missed 4 free throws the entire game. Even though Dwight Howard was one of the worst free throw shooters in the league he was able to hit 12 out of 16 free throws that night. Howard put up a staggering performance of 40 points and 14 rebounds. LeBron went on to score 25 points, 7 rebounds, and 7 assists. It was a solid performance, but with home court advantage in their favor the Magic ended up defeating the Cavs 103 - 90.

Following the loss to the Magic, critics began to swarm LeBron and wonder if he would ever win a championship with the Cavs. Was he as good as everyone had once thought? Could he possibly be as good as Michael Jordan? Was he chasing an impossible goal? What would he do now? The questions kept on coming. No one was paying any attention to what LeBron had done for the Cavs franchise, they seemed more focused on the fact that he failed to get to the finals and win a ring. He had taken one of the worst franchises in the league and within 5 years managed to make them of the best teams in the East Conference. It was no question that LeBron was a leader and wanted that ring, but would he be able to make it happen with the Cavs or would he be stuck chasing something that was out of his reach?

2009- 2010 Season

Following the Cavs loss to the Magic, it was obvious that they got beat by speed and shooting efficiency. Every year the Cavs had added new players to address weaknesses in their lineup. On the defensive end the previous year they added Ben Wallace to help establish a solid baseline defense. They also added a point guard Mo Williams who was in the midst of his prime. The Cavs had been trying to build a team around James and often times that was their most scrutinized mistake. It wasn't the right way to build a winning team. It was no question that James was a superstar, but it is extremely difficult to build a championship team around a single player.

The 2009 - 2010 NBA season was a big year for the league. There were a ton of superstars that could declared free agency and many people wondered if LeBron would end up doing the same. Many teams were trying to keep their superstars happy by giving them fat contracts and guarantees and a few teams had their sights set on LeBron. The Cavs needed to fix some of the weaknesses in their lineup that caused them to lose to the Magic the previous year. They added Anthony Parker, Antawn Jamison and the self-proclaimed superman himself, Shaquielle O'Neal to their roster. Anthony Parker was a veteran player who was a consistent three-point shooter from the Toronto Raptors. His addition to the Cavs would help improve the outside shooting they lacked the previous season. Antawn Jamison was brought on to improve their defensive mobility and to create more space on the offensive end. Shaq was brought on because he is Shaq. His basketball resume would need to have its own book created. Their goal was to have Shaq in the paint to slow down big players like Dwight Howard in tough games. The Cavs began to look like an actual team that didn't need to revolve strictly around James to be successful. They were more flexible on the offensive and defensive end than ever before. This was the season they had to become a championship team. a

The Cavaliers dominated their regular season and

finished with a 61-21 record. They were the number one team in the Eastern Conference. LeBron averaged 29.7 points, 7.3 rebounds and 8.6 assists per game. He would also go on to receive his second straight league MVP award. There are very few players that have received the league MVP award twice, let alone 2 consecutive years. The Cavs had performed better than they had in any other season.

The Cavs got off to a hot start in the 2010 playoffs. They were matched up with one of the worst teams that year, the Chicago Bulls. The Cavs ended up beating the Bulls 4-1 in their playoff series and waited on the outcome of Celtics and the Heat to see who they would play next. The Celtics ended up beating the Miami Heat 4-1. The Celtics had a very dynamic and aggressive team. Kevin Garnett led the passion and energy of the Celtics. Point guard Rajan Rondo led the floor and set a very fast style of play for the Celtics. Veteran Ray Allen, one of the best three-point shooters to ever play the game, drained 3's from anywhere he wanted to. Glen Davis played power forward and was a very aggressive defensive player who fought for every basket. Paul Pierce would do everything from drive the lane, dish it outside and hit game winning jump shots. They were no longer the "Big 3", they were the "Big 5". This would be the rematch the Cavs had been waiting for.

In Game 1 against the Celtics, LeBron put up 35 points, 7 rebounds and 7 assists. The Cavs came out victorious and beat the Celtics 101-93 at home. Their second game was also at home and it could put them at a huge advantage early on if they won. Unfortunately, the Celtics were the stronger team in Game 2 and defeated the Cavs 104-86. It was an embarrassing loss at home for the Cavs. The next game was away at the Boston Garden and people began to wonder if the Cavs still had it in them. In Game 3 the Cavs answered back and absolutely blew out the Celtics with a 124-95 win. LeBron dropped a staggering 38 points, 8 rebounds and 7 assists. That quickly shut most critics up. Despite their big loss, the Celtics remained calm and were able to win Game 4. The series were now tied up and it was very unclear who would end up winning at this point. This could be the last chance LeBron could have with the Cavs to win a championship and his career stood a major tipping point. Game 5 ended up being the worst playoff performance for James and the Cavs. The Celtics held LeBron to a mere 15 points, making only 3 of 14 field goal attempts. The Cavs ended up getting completely blown out in Game 5 losing by 32 points with a final score of 120-88. James and his team performed extremely sloppy and fans and critics definitely took notice. Game 6 would end up being one of the most important games of James's career as it would go on to change the course of his future.

Game 6 was an extremely close game. The Cavs and the Celtics were going back and forth every possession until the Celtics began to pull away in the third quarter. It was the sharpshooting of Ray Allen along with Paul Pierce that gave them a firm lead in the third. The Cavs would make a final comeback early in the 4th quarter but it wouldn't be enough to win the game. The Celtics ended up winning Game 6 with a final score of 94-85. LeBron put up an impressive triple double night with 27 points, 19 rebounds and 10 assists, but it didn't mean much when the team lost their final chance a title run that season. At the end of the game James simply disappeared into the locker without saying a word to anyone. No one knew what was going on with him at that point and if that would be the last time he would show up in a Cavaliers jersey. Shortly after that he began receiving major scrutiny from fans, critics and the media. They coined his prompt departure from Game 6 as his **"disappearing act"**.

Media analysts continued to put James on blast and scrutinize the way he left Game 6 and left many to wonder what that meant for the Cavaliers franchise. It was no question that the Cavs performed poorly in Game 6, but their leader was nowhere to be found when the questions from everyone came pouring in. How would the King respond?

Chapter 5 : The Change

It was clear to everyone that James wanted to leave a basketball legacy that would be remembered for years to come. The real question was, would he be able to build that legacy with the Cavaliers? Which team would be able to offer the right opportunity for James to maximize his talents? Would the Cavs become a championship team or continue to chase something that was out of their reach?

There were questions and uncertainties about LeBron and the Cavaliers flying from every angle. LeBron had to make a decision that would be best not only for him but also for his family. Going into the free agency, LeBron had a plethora of different options and teams that were ready to offer him a sizeable contract. All the top tier NBA teams like the New York Knicks, New Jersey Nets, Chicago Bulls, LA Clippers, Miami Heat were ready to make LeBron offers. Not only could each team offer LeBron millions of dollars, they also had their own star players that wouldn't require the franchise to build solely around LeBron's talents. For example, the New York Knicks had recently signed the ferocious Amare Stoudemire who was at the height of his NBA career. That combo would be unstoppable. The Chicago Bulls had a young team of Derrick Rose, Luol Deng, and Joakim Noah. Having a young team could present its own set of challenges, but also the potential for long term success if the they proved to be a good match. It would also mean that LeBron would play on the same team the great Michael Jordan played on. The critics and fans often compared LeBron to MJ and the possibility of playing for the Bulls was enticing. The LA Clippers were also a very interesting possibility as they were a struggling franchise. The idea of LeBron coming to their rescue was something many fans hoped for. But would LeBron really want to go through the struggles and pains of trying to rebuild a failing franchise? It was clear that LeBron had a central focus to be on a team that wanted to win a championship. There was something different about the Miami Heat and LeBron began to sense that they could be the best fit.

The Miami Heat were not a team that had the same historical accomplishments as some of the older franchises like the New York Knicks and the Chicago Bulls. They did however share a vision that was in line with LeBron's. They wanted to create a championship team. The Miami Heat had competent and experienced staff that was ready to do whatever was necessary to create an unstoppable franchise. In previous history, the Miami Heat had Pat Riley as their head coach, who had a strong history of building championship teams. He was widely regarded as one of the best coaches of all time. The Heat also had all-star point guard Dwyane Wade. He had major experience in the playoffs and in the finals and had also won a championship with Miami in 2006. During the free agency in 2010, Chris Bosh joined the Miami Heat roster. The Miami Heat were expanding their franchise into a powerhouse and if LeBron jumped on the team he could be the leading force that would push them to a championship.

The Cavaliers wanted to retain LeBron and made him a massive 30 million a year salary offer. They also tried to get Chris Bosh on the team during his free agency to strengthen up the Cavaliers potential, but that didn't end up working out. The Cavs hopes for keeping LeBron in his hometown were wearing thin. Would the King really leave his hometown and everything that he built? Many sources reported that James actually wanted to remain in Cleveland, but would he be willing to sacrifice another year chasing a championship that was out of his reach?

The Miami Heat offered LeBron something that other organizations simply couldn't. They offered him the best chance to win a championship. With coach Pat Riley who had won numerous championships in the past and with Miami Heat point guard Dwyane Wade who had recently won a championship in 2006, the Miami Heat seemed like the best fit for LeBron. They had the missing pieces LeBron was searching for. A winning mentality and attitude from Pat Riley and experienced championship point guard Dwyane Wade.

On July 8th, 2010 on ESPN, LeBron made his official decision and announcement to the world. *"In*

this fall I'm going to take my talents to South Beach and join the Miami Heat". Shortly after LeBron's announcement and decision was made, critics and fans went absolutely wild. They began to slam LeBron as being weak, uncommitted, and even calling him an average player. The backlash he received from hometown fans was some of the worst in sports history. Fans began burning his jersey, throwing rocks at his billboards, and so much more. Hometown fans slowly began portraying him as a villain. He was one of the most liked athletes in the world, but with his decision to leave the Cavs, he became one of the most hated and scrutinized players of all time. The Cavs owner Dan Gilbert, ended up writing a personal letter to LeBron calling him all sorts of names. He went on to even say that the Cavaliers would win a championship without LeBron on the team.

Despite the major backlash that LeBron received, it was the right decision for him at the time. He was now on a team that was built to succeed for years to come. LeBron's future with the Miami Heat was looking bright.

2010-2011 Season

Coming into the 2010-2011 season, LeBron was the most talked about player in the league. He was heavily scrutinized heading into the season and many people hoped he wouldn't go on to win a championship with the Heat. LeBron wasn't the only superstar player that left his team. Carmelo Anthony left the Denver Nuggets and Dwight Howard left the Orlando Magic. Why was LeBron receiving the kind of backlash from critics and fans while other players were treated fairly for leaving? The city of Cleveland saw LeBron as their hometown hero and savior, their own sports icon. When he left, fans felt like he had turned his back on the city that he came from. It was a more personal touch with James. In an interview, James was asked what he thought about the Miami Heat and what they would accomplish. James went on to say that he strongly believed that they would win multiple rings. This further fueled the fan fire and it was evident in most of the away games that the Heat had that season. Fans would boo James at the free throw line and say derogatory things to him as he entered the locker room. LeBron knew that he would face the criticism that came with his decision, but it wasn't as brutal as he had expected.

To add further pressure to the burning fire, the Heat started off their season very poorly. Nearly twenty games in their first season together the Heat started with a 9-8 Record. It quickly became one of the most talked about things in the NBA. LeBron was slowly adjusting to the style of play of his teammates. They slowly began to work in tandem with each other and started blowing teams away midway through the season. Chris Bosh, Dwyane Wade and LeBron James begin to click on and off the court and became unstoppable. LeBron slowly realized that he could rely on his teammates more and didn't have to be in full charge of the game. When games got tough he could rely on the speed and agility of Dwyane to get to the basket and do damage. He could rely on Bosh to play both a dynamic power forward and strong center depending on who they faced. The three of them were so versatile that they began to win games with ease which slowly erased the criticism. The critics wanted to see the Heat fall, but they did just the opposite. In his first season with the Miami Heat, LeBron averaged 26.7 points, 7.5 rebounds and 7 assists per game. He was getting closer and closer to averaging a triple double. During the middle of the season the Heat had a team meeting. They discussed the importance of their first season together and that they needed concentrate harder on winning more games. They began to turn things around and managed to win 21 of their next 22 games. It was a testament to their dedication to become the best team in the Eastern Conference that season. As the season continued to progress, the Miami Heat continued to improve under LeBron's leadership. In the month of February in 2011, LeBron went on to have the best performance of his career. He dropped 51 points, 11 rebounds and 8 assists. It was a stellar performance.

When the All-Star weekend came around, James, Bosh and Wade were selected to be part of the 2011

All-Star team. It was a huge accomplishment to have 3 All-Stars coming from the same team. The East ended up losing the All-Star game 143-148 to the West that year and Kobe was named the All-Star MVP. The Heat continued to play hard the rest of the season after the playoffs and managed to finish the season with a 58-24 record. Despite starting off shaky in the beginning of the season, the Heat turned things around and were ranked the number 2 team in the Eastern Conference behind the Chicago Bulls. The Bulls had one of their best seasons since MJ with a 62-20 record. This season the league MVP award ended up going to young Bulls point guard Derrick Rose.

It was now time for the Miami Heat to step up and perform in the playoffs. Going into the 2011 playoffs, critics were very hateful towards LeBron James and the Heat. It was no questions that fans wanted to see the Miami Heat go into downward spiral during the playoffs. The Heat faced the Philadelphia 76'ers in the first round. They quickly proved that they meant business and beat the Sixers in 5 games.

Their next matchup proved how good they really were. Their next opponent was a team which LeBron was very familiar with, the Boston Celtics. The Celtics had their own history with James in previous playoffs bouts. LeBron knew their game very well and was determined not to let things repeat. The Heat played some of the most exciting basketball that fans had seen. The Celtics big 3 was no match for Miami. Even though the Celtics had the experience and tenacity necessary to win, LeBron James and the Heat simply wore them down. The Heat ended up winning the series in 5 games. People began to talk that this could be the year that LeBron ends up winning his first ring. Next up were the Chicago Bulls.

It was a huge accomplishment by league MVP Derrick Rose to get his team to the Eastern Conference finals. He was an absolute star in the playoffs. Rose was a serious threat to the Heat because he was such an explosive point guard. He could shoot from the outside and penetrate the rim with absurd speed. The Bulls were a great defensive team and it was no doubt that the series would be fun to watch. The Heat ended up losing Game 1 against the Bulls 103-82. It was a complete blowout which had many analysts and fans confused. How could the Heat perform so poorly? LeBron had a terrible game with 15 points, 6 rebounds and 6 assists. The Bulls defensive was simply too much for the Heat in Game 1. Following their embarrassing Game 1 loss, the Heat needed to adjust their focus back to the original game plan, just win games.

There were some serious questions going around the Heat and their inability to beat the Bulls. Game 2 started off poorly for the Heat with the Bulls outscoring the Heat 26-19 at the end of the first quarter. LeBron was determined to win and it showed in the second half of the game. LeBron led the Heat with 29 points, 10 rebounds and 5 assists and was the driving force in the fourth quarter to help the Heat get the win. The Heat allowed only 10 points to the Bulls in the fourth quarter and LeBron scored 9 out of his 29 points in the final 5 minutes of the fourth quarter. LeBron was the major factor in helping the Heat with Game 2 as he shifted his focus on defending the lightning fast Derrick Rose. The Heat would end up winning Game 3 with a final score of 96-85. LeBron focused on driving to the lane more in Game 3 to force Chicago into early foul trouble. It also allowed him to dish it out to Bosh more as he drove to lane which ended up creating additional scoring possibilities for the team. Bosh went on to have a career post-season high of 34 points in Game 3. LeBron was also able to shut down Derrick Rose defensively in the fourth quarter and force him to take off-balance shots.

Game 4 was another high-pressure game where things were once again in LeBron's hands. Dwyane Wade struggled most of the game but LeBron and Bosh came through. LeBron Had 35 points, 6 rebounds and 6 assists. Bosh chimed in with 22 points, 10 rebounds and 1 assist. Game 4 ended up going into overtime and James had to deliver. In overtime LeBron shut down Derrick Rose defensively and the Heat ended up winning the game 101- 93. The Heat were only one game away from becoming Eastern Conference Champions and heading to the finals.

In Game 5 LeBron went on to score 28 points, 11 rebounds and 6 assists to help the Heat beat the Bulls 83-80. The Heat became Eastern Conference Champions and were heading into the finals. The Heat stood to face the Dallas Mavericks in the finals who were a premier team that always managed to get far in the playoffs. Could this finally be the year that LeBron wins his first championship? The Dallas Mavericks were an experienced finals team and were ready to do anything to win that championship.

In Game 1 of the 2011 NBA finals LeBron had 24 points, 9 rebounds and 5 assists. LeBron had good a shooting night behind the arc, hitting 4 out of his 5 three pointers for the night. The Heat went on to win Game 1 with a final score of 92-84. LeBron was beginning to taste that championship. Game 2 was an entirely different game for the Heat. Dwyane Wade had an incredible Game 2 with 36 points, 5 rebounds and 6 assists. The Heat were looking good in the 4th quarter with an 88-73 lead over the Mavericks with a little over

8 minutes remaining. The Heat felt like they had the game in the bag. What happened in the next 8 minutes baffled fans and everyone watching the game. The Dallas Mavericks began scoring frantically in the last 8 minutes and the Heat had trouble answering back. The Heat began to break down defensively in the 4th quarter and the Dallas Mavericks ended up winning the game 95-93. People couldn't believe that the Heat lost game 2. They needed to seriously concentrate. This was the NBA finals. You can't let your guard slip up for even one minute, let alone eight minutes.

The Heat needed to regain their focus and perform in Game 3. In Game 3 LeBron had an average performance with 17 points, 3 rebounds and 9 assists on a 6 of 14 shooting. Dwyane Wade ended up having a clutch performance with 29 points, 11 rebound and 3 assists. Was the pressure of the finals too much for LeBron to handle at this point? Chris Bosh and Dwyane Wade picked up the slack for LeBron's performance and helped carry the team to a win with Chris Bosh hitting the game winning shot. The Heat won Game 3 with a final score of 88-86.

Game 4 was another extremely close game and one of the worst performances of LeBron's career. The Mavericks held LeBron to 8 points, 9 rebounds and 7 assists. It couldn't have gone much worse for LeBron in Game 4. They simply shut him down defensively and LeBron could not get any shots to Fall. The Heat went on to lose Game 4 with a final score of 86-83. If LeBron performed even halfway decent the Heat could have most likely won Game 4. LeBron had half as many turnovers as he did points. He needed to seriously improve his performance or they would lose the title. The series were now tied up at 2-2 and it was unclear at this point as to who would win the 2011 NBA championship. The pressure to perform was on and James needed to bounce back in Game 5 if he was serious about winning a championship.

In Game 5 James had a solid performance with a triple double consisting of 17 points, 10 rebounds and 10 assists. LeBron started off the first half very aggressive, but ended the rest of the game very passively. He did not attack the paint like he did in the first half and limited himself to poor jump shots. Dallas's zone defense was too much for James and the Heat. The team failed to adjust to it and as a result up lost Game 5 with a final score of 112-103. Things were not looking good for the Heat.

The Heat were down 3-2 and it was now time for LeBron to perform and show the world why he was *"The Chosen One"*. Game 6 started off hot for LeBron. He hit his first four shots and scored nine points to give the Heat an early 20-11 lead. Even though LeBron started off hot, he would go on to score only 12 points the rest of the game. It began to look like he was giving up again like Game 3. He was taking poor shots and was not driving down the lane as much as he needed to in order to be effective. The Mavericks simply played better than the Heat. They distributed the ball effectively and made key defensive stops when they mattered. LeBron ended the game with 21 points, 4 rebounds and 6 assists. The Heat ended up losing Game 6 with a final score of 105 – 95. The Dallas Mavericks had become the 2011 NBA Champions.

It was a depressing way to lose the finals the way they did and LeBron knew he and the team had some serious work to do in the offseason. As usual, the hypothetical what-ifs came pouring in from sports commentators, analysts and critics following the Heat's loss to the Mavericks. It was no question that the Mavericks were a tough team to beat. There were so many ways that the Heat underperformed it left many to question if they even cared about winning a championship and if LeBron could respond to the pressure of the finals. Would LeBron be able to finally win a championship next season, or would he be stuck chasing a dream that was far out of his reach?

2011- 2012 Season

It was no question that the Miami Heat were a talented Team. They had made it all the way to the NBA finals and that in itself a major accomplishment. The way the Big 3 started to fall apart in the finals sparked many questions regarding their chemistry. With LeBron's embarrassing performance in Game 4 people began to questions whether he could handle the pressure that comes with the finals. This wasn't the first time LeBron had begun to crumble during a finals bout, and many critics wondered if the King would ever win a championship. Even though the Miami Heat had a great regular season the previous year and got to the finals, it really didn't matter. People were so focused on the fact that LeBron had blown his chance to win a title that his other accomplishments began to get overlooked. In the weeks following the finals, LeBron completely isolated himself from everyone to reflect on what had gone wrong. LeBron had to dig deep to reflect not only on his performance, but the whole dynamic of the team. LeBron knew he wouldn't be able to win a championship by himself. If he could improve the chemistry of the team the Heat would have a much better chance of winning the title. Feeling the weight of the loss, Dwyane Wade reached out to LeBron so they could sit down and come up with a strategy that would push them to win a title. Dwyane Wade suggested that LeBron be the main leader of the team. Bosh, James and Wade were already the main players of the team, but they never established a main leader the previous season. Dwyane Wade felt that this was their primary downfall. The Heat needed LeBron to be who he was for the Cavaliers. They needed LeBron to be the leading force of the team, the visionary, and the person who would push the entire team to strive for greatness. After he cleared his mind of the past and with a new focus set forth, LeBron was ready to mold a new reality. He wasn't just ready to play basketball to win games, he was ready to strive for greatness.

With a new mentality and focus the Heat were ready to win a championship this year. They made some small changes in their lineup that improved their team dynamic. They brought on veteran player Shane Battier to help improve their starting 5 lineup. Battier not only had the experience, but he had also had a leadership mentality that focused on constant team improvement. He was a great leader with the Rockets and the Grizzlies and would help the Heat keep their composure in high pressure game situations.

The Heats 2011-2012 season would be put on pause due to the NBA lockout that was going on that year. The 2011 NBA lockout was the 4th lockout ever in NBA history. The lockout lasted 161 days starting from July 1 to Dec 8. The main issues related to the lockout was the division of revenue and how the salary cap and luxury tax was structured. The proposal from the owners wanted to reduce the share of player related income from 57% down to 47%. The counter offer from the players was 53%. The owners fought back and wanted to put a hard salary cap and luxury tax on players in hopes of increasing the competition between franchises. Both sides eventually ended up failing to reach an agreement which resulted in the NBA canceling all pre-season games through December. On November 26, they ended up reaching an agreement that would end the lockout. They came to an agreement of a revenue split of 49% -51.2% and a flexible salary cap, but with a harsher luxury tax enforcement.

Even though the lockout was going on, LeBron and the Heat continued to go hard and improve on every angle of their game. On opening day after the lockout, LeBron proved why he was the King. He put up 37 points, 10 rebounds and 6 assists against the team that had beaten them in the finals, the Mavericks. Despite a shortened season the team was playing much better than the previous season. They had a consistent tempo and managed to control the flow of each game. At the end of the regular season LeBron averaged 27.1 points, 7.9 rebounds and 6.2 assists per game. He improved as a leader and the team ended the season with a 46-20 record. LeBron also ended up getting his third MVP award that season. Things were aligning for LeBron and the Heat and it was time for the playoffs to begin once again. They knew they could get to the finals, but this time they couldn't let up. They had to stay consistent and perform all the way through.

In their first round of playoffs that season the Heat went on to face the New York Knicks. The Heat ended up beating them in five games and made it seem very effortless as they won each game by more than 10 points. Their intensity and focus on another level. In their second round of playoffs they went on to face the Indiana Pacers. In Game 1 against the Pacers LeBron put up 32 points, 15 rebounds and 5 assists. He led his team to a 95-86 win. The next two games Indiana picked up their intensity and beat the Heat. LeBron seriously needed to evaluate the team's strategy or they could end up with an early exit. In Game 4 the team came together and beat the Pacers 101-93. The Heat went on to win the Game 5 and 6 in complete blowouts. They crushed the Pacers 115-83 in Game 5 and 105-93 in Game 6. They were hungry for that championship. In Game 4 everyone saw why LeBron was the King as he poured in 40 points, 18 rebounds and 9 assists. Just one assist shy of a nasty playoff triple double.

The Heat would go on to face the Celtics in the Eastern Conference Finals. It would be one of the most epic showdowns in playoff history. A performance of the decades. Game 1 against the Celtics ended up being a total blowout with the Heat winning 93-79. The Heat dominated on all ends of the floor. LeBron dropped 32 points, 13 rebounds and 3 assists. Dwyane Wade had a solid performance with 22 points, 7 assists and 3 boards. Game 2 ended up being a tight game, but the Heat came out and won the game. The finals score was 115-111. They were getting closer and closer to getting to the finals again. Game 3 would prove to be a challenge for the Heat and the Celtics ended up beating them 101-91. Game 4 ended up being a very close game and both teams played exceptional offense and defense. LeBron finished the game with 29 points, 6 rebounds and 3 assists. Dwyane Wade also had a solid game with 20 points, 7 rebounds and 6 assists. Even though it was a close game the Heat ended up losing 93-91. The series were now tied 2-2 and the pressure was turning up for the Heat. The Celtics were not going to let up and the Heat seriously needed to strategies to beat them. Game 5 was another close game. LeBron played his heart out and scored 30 points, 13 rebounds and 2 assists. His efforts would not be enough and they went on to lose Game 5 with a final score of 94-90. The Heat were now one game away from losing the whole series. If they wanted that championship they had to look to their leader. LeBron had to deliver in Game 6 or they would be sent home packing. In Game 6 LeBron had one of the best playoff performances of his career, pouring in 45 points, 15 rebounds and 5 assists. He simply refused to lose and carried the Heat to a 98-79 victory. It was now off to Game 7 and the pressure and stakes were higher than ever. Would LeBron be able to lead his team to a win over the Celtics so they could advance to the finals?

Everyone began to scrutinize and predict that LeBron would choke under the pressure. LeBron didn't care about the critics that doubted him and was solely focused on helping to push his team to a win. In Game 7 LeBron was relentless getting to the rim. He scored 31 points, 12 rebounds and 2 assists. Dwyane Wade had 23 points, 6 rebounds and 6 assists. The game started off slow, but things began to pick up in the 2nd quarter. It was a close game heading into the second half until the Heat began to slowly pull away and shut down the Celtics defensively. Chris Bosh was clutch from the 3 point line in the 3rd and 4th quarter and the Heat managed to power through and come out with the win. The final score of the game was 101-88. The Heat were once again headed to the NBA finals.

LeBron was focused and determined to not let the championship slip past him this year. The Heat were playing like a championship team and they were once again where they wanted to be, the finals. They were facing the Oklahoma City Thunder in the finals with a young rising star Kevin Durant who could do it all. He could shoot from practically anywhere he wanted to, drive the lane, score effortlessly and be a defensive threat. He would prove to a be a tough matchup for LeBron and it was no questions that the finals were going to be full of stellar performances and competition. The Thunder also had Russell Westbrook as their point guard who was explosive, aggressive and would do anything to win. Durant and Westbrook were both All-Star players who wanted to win just as bad as LeBron. The real question was, who was going to win and become the 2012 NBA championship team?

Going into the finals it was unclear who would really win. In the regular season the series were tied up at 1-1. Both teams were so evenly stacked against each other that most analysts and experts couldn't really argue, but just wait to see how the finals would unfold. Game 1 started off with the fast pace style of play that the Thunder were used to playing. They were running the floor wide and getting to the basket aggressively. Kevin Durant had a killer performance with 36 points, 8 rebounds and 4 assists. He proved to be serious competition for LeBron. Westbrook would also go on to have a solid night with 27 points, 8 rebounds and 11 assists. LeBron ended Game 1 with 30 points, 9 rebounds and 4 assists. The Thunder proved to be the better team in Game 1 and ended up winning 105-94. It was the type of game that had cost them the championship in the past. LeBron was determined to not let that happen again. Game 2 would prove to be a tough game, but the Heat came out on top and won 100-96. It was an extremely close game and everyone could see that both teams were hungry for that championship. LeBron finished Game 2 with 32 points, 8 rebounds, and 5 assists. Dwyane Wade contributed 24 points to add to the Heats win. Game 3 was another battle for the two teams and the Heat came out on top again winning the game 91-85. The Heat were playing smart basketball and knew that if they tried to play at the pace that Westbrook and Durant were, they would be at a disadvantage. They saw this early on in Game 1 and decided to slow the flow of the game and throw the Thunder off their game. In Game 4 the Heat knew they had to do their best to keep their composure and control the flow of the game. If they did that they knew they were going to win. The game started of slow, but started to pick up in the second half of the with Westbrook getting aggressive driving to the basket.

Westbrook finished the night with 43 points, but the Heat managed to control the game in their favor and ended up winning 104-98. LeBron was not caving in and was proving to be a leader when things began to get tough. There were nearly 15 lead changes between the 3rd and 4th quarter, but LeBron saw that his team needed him to be a leader and step up. He finished the night with 26 points, 9 rebounds and 12 assists. One rebound away from a triple double. The Heat were now one game away from becoming NBA champions and LeBron was one game away from getting his first ring. So far, no team in NBA history has ever came back from a 3-1 deficit in the finals to win it. The Heat were no strangers to luck and Cinderella stories. They knew they were not going to let that happen. The Thunder needed a miracle to win. In Game 5 the Thunder looked defeated, tired and not ready to play. The Heat took full advantage and won 121- 106. LeBron played his heart out and finished the game with a triple double consisting of 26 points, 11 rebounds and 13 assists. The Heat became 2012 NBA champs and LeBron had finally won his first championship. The journey that LeBron had been on to finally win his first NBA championship was filled with many challenges, but he was finally a champion. After the game was over LeBron was up on stage next to one of the best basketball players of all time, Bill Russell and was awarded the *2012 NBA finals MVP* award. All of the hard work, sacrifices and public scrutiny he endured had paid off. LeBron James was finally an NBA champion.

2012-2013 Season

Following their championship win, the Miami Heat was the team that everyone wanted to beat. They now had a winning foundation and attitude to start the next season and get even better. People had been comparing LeBron to the great Michael Jordan ever since he came in the league. After winning his first title it was becoming a reality that he had the skills, determination and passion to be better than MJ. How would his success in the NBA be measured? Would it be by the amount of championship he won, the amount of points he scored, or the impact that he would have on the game of basketball? It was very unclear at this point, but what was clear is that LeBron was one of the best players in the league and he would continue his quest to strive for greatness.

In the 2012–2013 season, the Heat made some changes to their lineup in order to add some strength and versatility. They saw they lacked some outside shooting in the playoffs that could have cost them the championship. They needed a veteran player who was a clutch 3-point shooter and would not afraid to take a shot when the game is on the line. So why not bring on one of the best 3 point shooters of all time, Ray Allen. Ray Allen had won a championship with the Boston Celtics and had an obsessive work ethic that the Heat needed. He was the type of player the Heat needed if they wanted to win a championship back to back. As Chris Bosh got moved to the center position it meant that LeBron would have to transition to play as the power forward. Playing power forward would give him the opportunity to be more of a defensive threat and score inside the paint more. He could concentrate on getting more aggressive towards the basket and take higher percentage shots. Even though LeBron was used to playing small forward, his physical build was meant for a power forward. It was obvious that in certain situations LeBron would be a terrifying mismatch for many teams and it would help the Heat win more games. This new transition proved to be a total success as LeBron's player efficiency improved drastically. In the first 20 games of the regular season he didn't shoot below 50%. He was a lethal threat to other teams because he was scoring in different ways that matched his strengths. The Heat's new strategy worked so well that they ended up going on a 27- game winning streak. It would end up being the 2nd best regular season NBA streak of all time. At the end of the season LeBron averaged 26.8 points, 8 rebounds and 7.3 assists per game. He was taking smarter shots and playing like a leader. He ended the regular season with new career shooting high of 56.5%. The Heat finished their regular season with a 66-16 record and were ranked the number one team in the Eastern Conference. LeBron also ended up receiving his 4th MVP award. It was a true testament to his dedication to not only his team, but the game of basketball.

After such a successful regular season, it was time for the playoffs once again. The Heat were such a dominant team in the regular season and all people seemed to talk about was if they would be NBA champs again. Getting to the finals was nothing new for LeBron.

It was simply a question of whether or not he would win another championship.

The Heat played the Milwaukee Bucks in the first round of playoffs and beat them with ease in 4 games. In the Eastern Conference semifinals they face the Bulls and ended up beating them in 5 games. It was clear they meant business. They did however have some trouble against the Indiana Pacers in the Eastern Conference finals and ended up going to 7 games. Each game they played was very tight, but the Heat ended up beating them in Game 7 to advance to the NBA finals once again. They would go on to face the San Antonio Spurs. LeBron knew that the Spurs were a veteran team and would most likely end up going to 7 games. The Spurs were disciplined and played with a killer mentality.

The Spurs quickly set the tone in Game 1 with a 92-88 win over Miami. LeBron and the Heat played extremely well, but the Spurs experience showed. In Game 2 the Heat stepped up and beat the Spurs with a final score of 103-84. Despite LeBron's average performance of only 17 points, the Heat managed to beat the Spurs in Game 2. In Game 3 at San Antonio, the Spurs completely shut down the Heat in an embarrassing loss of 113-77. They absolutely dismantled the Heat and LeBron could feel the pressure starting to build. The Heat knew they couldn't let those kind of blowout games happen any longer. The Spurs held LeBron to a measly 15 points, Dwayne Wade to 16 points, Chris Bosh to only 12 points and Ray Allen to 4. The experienced defense of the Spurs proved to be too much for the Heat. The Heat needed to pivot and rely on their leader to come forward and push them to victory. LeBron did just that in Game 4 and led the Heat to 109-93 win over the Spurs. LeBron had 33 points, 11 rebounds and 4 assists. LeBron was the type of leader that would not only have good games himself, but he would also elevate the game of his teammates. Dwayne Wade finished Game 4 with 32 points, Chris Bosh with 20 points, and Ray Allen with 14. It was evident that when LeBron performed well he managed to push the rest of his teammates to stellar performances as well. Game 5 was a complete and total battle in which the

Spurs came out victorious. They ended up winning 114-104 and the Heat were now one game away from losing the championship. Game 6 was an insanely close game, with over 10 lead changes in the 3rd quarter alone. The Heat were down 13 points in the 4th quarter and LeBron pushed and managed to even up the score. The game ended up going to overtime and LeBron needed to step up and perform or the Heat would be sent home packing. With 55.4 second remaining in overtime the Heat were up 101-100. No one could get an easy shot as both teams were playing with laser focus. The whole crowd was silent and waiting for that last minute of the game to be over which seemed like an eternity. With a strong drive to the basket with less than 10 seconds to go Manu Ginobili drove it down the lane looking to get fouled, but ended up getting the ball stripped away. The ball ended up in Ray Allen's hands and the Spurs had nothing left to do but foul him. With no fouls left to give Ray Allen headed to the free throw line where he would sink the two free throws to put the Heat up 103-100. After Ray Allen sunk both free throws the Spurs only had

1.9 seconds remaining. The Spurs inbounded the ball to Danny Green in the corner where he would try to sink a three to tie the game, but would end up getting blocked blocked by Chris Bosh. The Heat had barely managed to win the game, but were now headed to Game 7 for the championship. It was one of those defining games for the Heat to come back and force the overtime and force a Game 7. LeBron ended the game with a triple double consisting of 32 points, 10 rebounds and 11 assists.

Game 7 was a home game for the Heat and they simply had no choice but to win. The game started off slow and both teams were playing extremely close defense. In the first 6 minutes of the first quarter the score was 11-4. Each team was fighting for every point they scored. At the end of the first quarter the score was 18-16 with Miami in the lead. It was a battle for the championship and one of the most intense NBA finals of all time. At the end of the first half the score of the game was 46-44 with Miami in the lead. At the half LeBron had to dig deep and determine what he needed to do to take his team to victory.

LeBron went on to have a big 3rd quarter with 13 points. The Heat found Kawhi Leonard to be a problem in the 3rd quarter as he went on to score 9 points by aggressively driving to the basket. With 5.2 seconds to go in the third quarter the Heat inbounded the ball to Mario Chalmers who dribbled fast across the court and launched a thirty-footer off the backboard to end the third quarter 72-71 and give Miami a one point lead. The fourth quarter was an absolute bloodbath. San Antonio went on to have 5 turnovers in the first 11 possessions which ended up putting the Heat up 81-77 in the first 6 minutes. With 4 minute and 25 seconds remaining in the 4th, Manu Ginobili sank a three to cut Miami's lead to three points. The score was now 85-82. Three possessions later neither team had scored until LeBron found Shane Battier wide open at the corner for a three that he sunk which put the Heat up 88-82. Shane Battier had a huge night on a 6-8 shooting from downtown. The two teams went back to back with Kawhi Leondard hitting a three to cut the Heat's lead to 2 points. The score was now 90-88 with only two minutes remaining. The Spurs shooting was terrible in the fourth quarter with 6-20 and a total of 7 turnovers. With 30 seconds remaining in the 4th LeBron had the ball at the top of the key, dribbled in and took a shot at the top of the right corner of the free throw line. He sunk the shot which put the Heat up by 4 points. The Spurs failed to score again and the Heat ended up winning the game 95-88. They had done it once again. They had won the 2013 NBA championship. LeBron was once again crowned the NBA finals MVP. LeBron finished the night with 37 points, 12 rebounds and 4 assists. It was an unbelievable achievement for the Heat to win back to back titles. LeBron had elevated his NBA career to new heights and achieved the impossible. What would happen next season? Could the Heat 3-peat and win yet another title?

2013-2014 Season

People who once doubted LeBron quickly shut up following the Heats back to back title wins. He now had 2 rings on his finger and clutch performances in the finals games to back them up. His doubters and skeptics were now his fans and supporters. The Heat didn't make a ton of changes to their lineup this season. The new additions to their team would include Michael Beasley and Greg Oden. This season would prove to be different for James.

James had to do more for the team this year due to Dwayne Wade missing roughly 30 games of the regular season. Dwayne Wade began to experience problems with his knees which caused him to miss more games than anyone expected. This led to some struggles for the Heat during their regular season. However, LeBron didn't let that hurdle stop him from having an amazing regular season. LeBron averaged 27.1 points, 6.9 rebounds and 6.3 assists this season. He went on to have a new career high of 61 points against the

Charlotte Bobcats. LeBron's 61 points ended up being a franchise-high, beating Glen Rice's record of 56 points in 1995. The Heat finished the regular season with a 54-28 record. Not quite as impressive as their previous season, but still a solid performance. They were back in the playoffs and it was time to battle again.

In the first round of their playoff series the Heat faced the Charlotte Bobcats. They quickly swept the Bobcats in 4 games and advanced to round two to face Brooklyn Nets. They quickly beat the Nets in 5 games and advanced against their previous year's rivals, the Indiana Pacers. The Pacers ended up giving the Heat a run for their money and took them to 6 games before the Heat won. LeBron went on to have his worst playoff performance of his career in Game 5 scoring only 7 points. They proved to be a tough opponent, but the Heat managed to come out with a win. The Heat had now won their fourth consecutive Eastern Conference championship and became the first team to do so since the 1986-87 Boston Celtics. They were once again headed to the NBA finals to face the San Antonio Spurs.

This was the Heats chance to make NBA history and win 3 consecutive championships.

The Spurs had different plans for the Heat this time around. They were determined to not let the Heat have a comeback the way they did the previous year. The change in the Spurs defense was obvious this time around as they set the tone in Game 1 and beat Miami by 15 points. They kept LeBron off the boards on the offensive end and limited their penetration to the basket with a zone defense. This caused the Heat to take more contested shots from the outside which they had trouble making. Game 2 ended up being a close game and the Heat came out ahead and won Game 2 with a final score of 98-96. The Heat knew they were going to struggle against the Spurs this time around as other members of the team were finding it more and more difficult to score. The next 3 games that followed were an absolute massacre. The Spurs would go on to beat the Heat in the next 3 games by a huge margin of over 15 points in each game. Even though LeBron had stellar performances in those games, the Spurs defense was too strong for them this time around. The Spurs kept their mistakes to a low minimum this time. Last time they played the Heat they had turnover after turnover, but this time they played controlled basketball and managed to force the Heat to take poor shots which caused their defeat. A major factor in the Spurs win was the improvement in Kawhi Leondard's overall game. He was a threat both on the offensive and defensive ends of the floor. The Heat accepted the loss with great sportsmanship and knew that the Spurs were simply the better team this time around. Would the Heat continue their journey to fight for more championship? What was LeBron going to do next? Did he have a yearning to return back to his hometown of Ohio and get the championship that he always wanted? The questions were flying all over the board, but the decision was LeBron's.

Chapter 6: I'm coming Home

Following the Heat's loss to the Spurs, LeBron was a free agent and there was a ton of speculation as to what he was going to do. Many people believed that he would resign with the Heat due to the success he had with them and the bond he built with Chris Bosh and Dwayne Wade. He could stay in Miami and try to chase more championships with the Big 3 or he could return home to Cleveland, revive the city and bring home a championship. The speculations from the media and analysts all pointed to LeBron returning home to Cleveland and they were correct.

2014-2015 Season

LeBron made his final decision to return home to Cleveland. The fans of Cleveland were fired up and ready to have their king return to where he belonged. LeBron returned to Cleveland as a more mature leader and player. He knew that raw talent alone would not be enough to help bring a championship to the city of Cleveland. He knew he needed a team to share the vision with him and be ready to put in the kind of work that would mold a team into champions. The kind of work that requires sacrifice and a willingness to improve on every facet of the game.

In the weeks following LeBron's announcement of his return to the city of Cleveland, talks of acquiring Kevin Love began to surface. Their plan was to have a triple threat in Cleveland consisting of LeBron, Kevin Love and one of the best point guards in the league, Kyrie Irving. After much speculation, the Cavs made it official that Kevin Love was going to join them in the 2014 season. The Cleveland Cavaliers were looking good with LeBron, Kevin Love and Kyrie Irving being the leaders of the team. It was now time for James to work hard to bring home a championship to the city of Cleveland. LeBron James a.k.a *"The Chosen One"*, a.k.a the *"Kid from Akron"* was back in his hometown and willing to put it all on the line for his city.

LeBron's first game back to the city of Cleveland would be nothing short of legendary. Over 20,000 loyal fans greeted LeBron as he walked back in through the tunnels of the Quicken Loans arena. LeBron and the Cavs received a standing ovation on their way in and it was one of the most memorable times of LeBron's career. The fans and the city of Cleveland were ready for their king to return home. The whole first quarter of the game the fans were intense and cheering on LeBron every single time he got the ball in his hands. The Cavs faced the New York Knicks for their season opener and despite losing 95-90 , the energy that came from fans and players set the tone for the rest of their season. Even though the Cavs lost their season opener, the king was back and ready to fulfill his promise to the city of

Cleveland and bring home that championship.

The Cavs went on to have a slow start to their regular season losing 3 of their first 5 games and then losing four consecutive games between their 9th and 12th game. This sparked a ton of criticism from sports commentators and analysts. They began to say that the Cavs simply didn't have it in them and that LeBron was not the leader that he was in Miami. The Cavs would eventually turn things around and win 8 consecutive games following their losses. They began to play more in sync with each other and things began to look good for them. Thirty games into the regular season LeBron began to experience some muscle strains in his lower back and pain in his knees. It that caused him to miss 8 games between December 30th of 2014 and January 11th of 2015. During LeBron's 8 game absence, the Cavs played terribly and lost 7 of those games. His absence proved how much the Cavs needed him to win. After he returned from his injury the Cavs went on to win 11 games in a row. It was obvious that LeBron's presence on the court was needed in order for the Cavs to perform at their peak.

Around the same time that LeBron returned from his injury the Cavs ended up acquiring shooting guard Iman Shumpert from the Knicks. Iman Shumpert was the type of defensive player that the Cavs needed. They needed someone who could defend players around the perimeter, and Shumpert would go on to fill that void. They also ended up acquiring J.R. Smith from the Knicks, an athletic small guard who could shoot from the three, drive aggressively to the lane and defend like no other. They boosted their lineup and were hungrier than ever to go after the title. They would go on to finish the regular season with a 53-29 record. They finished first in the NBA Central Division and second in the Eastern Conference. People began to wonder what would happen to the Cavs if LeBron began to suffer the same injuries in the playoffs. Even though it wasn't the kind of record that LeBron was hoping for, the Cavs stood confident and ready for the playoffs.

The Cavs went on to face the Boston Celtics in their first round of playoffs and swept them in four games. The Cavs were playing like an All-Star team and did not have any trouble beating the Celtics. Their second round of playoffs were against an improved Chicago Bulls team who gave them a tough run. The Cavs would however emerge victorious and beat them in six games. Their next series against the Atlanta Hawks was projected to be a tough, but the Cavs ended up sweeping them in four games. They ended up crushing them in Game 4 by 30 points and the way they played made everybody think that this was the year that they would win a championship.

The Cavs were in the finals facing the Golden State Warriors who were having one of their best seasons in franchise history. The Warriors relied on their fast ball movement and consistent three-point shooting to win games. This made it very difficult for other teams to properly adjust on defense. Their style of play was extremely fast and efficient and teams simply crumbled against them. They often blew teams out by 20 to 30 point. One thing was for certain, the finals would between them and the Cavaliers would be a battle.

In Game 1 against the Warriors LeBron had an unforgettable night. He dropped 44 points, 8 rebound and 6 assists. The Warriors defense could not stop him. He made 18 of the 38 field goals he attempted and 2 of 8 three-pointers. Kyrie Irving finished the night with 23 points, 7 rebounds and 6 assists. With the last 2:20 left to go in the game the Cavaliers didn't expect what happened next. Kyrie Irving went down and started limping across the floor. He ended up leaving the game and headed straight to the locker room. Despite LeBron's stellar performance the Cavs came up short and lost Game 1 by 8 points. Following Game 1 news came out that Kyrie Irving would be out for the remainder of the finals due to a fractured kneecap. After the news was announced Kyrie sent the following message to his fans on Instagram. *"I want to thank everyone for the well wishes. Saddened by the way I had to go out but it doesn't take away from being a part of a special playoff run with my brothers. Truly means a lot for all the support and love. I gave it everything I had and have no regrets. I love this game no matter what and I'll be back soon. To my brothers: You already know what the deal is".* The Cavs star point guard would not be able to help them fight for the title this year and the pressure was once again all on LeBron. Even though Kyrie was out for the remainder of the finals, LeBron was determined to make a run for the title. In Game 2 he had an unforgettable triple double consisting of 39 points, 16 rebounds and 11 assists. The Cavs may have gotten lucky in Game 2 due to Steph Curry having a terrible shooting night. He made only 5 out of 23 field goals and 2 out of 15 three-pointers. The Cavs managed to beat the Warriors in overtime 95-93. In Game 3 Steph Curry had an incredible shooting night sinking 7 of 13 three-pointers and making 10 out of 20 field goals. LeBron also went on to have an amazing night dropping 40 points, 12 rebounds and 8 assists. He was only 2 assists shy of a back to back triple double. The Cavs managed to win Game 3 with a final score of 96-91. Despite not having their leading point guard, they were playing together and distributing the ball well. The Cavs had gained some momentum the last two games and hoped to carry it in Game 4. It was clear that Game 4 was going to be different right from the tip-off. The Warriors offense had turned stale in Games 2 and 3, but they shifted the tempo of their offense for more pick and rolls rather than the run and gun show they were used to. This caught the Cavaliers off guard and they failed to properly adjust their gameplay in order to win. They held LeBron to 20 points and ended up embarrassing the Cavaliers with a 103-82 win. It was clear that the Warriors had found a weakness in the Cavaliers defense and went on to take advantage of it. The Cavs and LeBron needed to adjust their style of play or they would be in serious trouble. LeBron went on to have a stellar triple double performance in Game 5, dropping 40 points, 14 rebounds and 11 assists. His performance would however come short to get the Cavaliers a win. Steph Curry was absolutely on fire from the field in Game 5, dropping 37 points. He made 7 out of the 13 three-pointers he attempted. Even though LeBron had a great performance in Game 5, the Warriors managed to beat them by 13 points. The final score of Game 5 was 104-91. The Cavs were now only one game away from letting the championship slide past them. They needed to adjust their style of play if they had any hopes of winning the championship. In Game 6 LeBron had 32 points, 18 rebounds and 9 assists. He had an absolutely star-studded performance, but the Cavaliers fell short and lost the game 105-97. The Warriors became the 2015 NBA champions. Despite the Cavs loss to Warriors LeBron's performance in the finals was one for the record books. He averaged 35.8 points, 13.3 rebounds and 8.8 assists. LeBron realized why the Cavs lost to the Warriors and was determined to not let it happen again. He knew that they failed to properly adjust their gameplay as a team. It was obvious to fans and analysts that the Cavs needed Kyrie Irving and LeBron playing together in order to win a championship. Would they be able to make it happen next year?

2015-2016 Season

The Cavaliers planned to make no changes to their lineup that got them to the finals the previous season. Even though the Cavs made it to the finals the past year, they began to crumble when the Warriors adjusted their style of play. This season, LeBron planned to improve the team dynamic between everyone in order to have the ability to adjust in any situation. LeBron recognized that the Cavs lacked a consistency factor when they gained momentum. He planned to work on that with the team in order to finally bring home a championship to Cleveland.

There were no other teams in the league like the Cavaliers and the Warriors. They were the two most championship-hungry teams and people strongly believed that they would see them battle again in the finals.

The Cavs started their season off hot by winning 15 of their first 20 games. Their improvement over the previous season was obvious to everyone who watched them play. The team was coming together and playing better than ever despite not having Kyrie Irving running the point. Kyrie returned on the 25th game of the season and was off to a good start following his finals injury. His first game back following his injury Cleveland faced the Philadelphia 76'ers. It was obvious how much better the Cavs played with Irving and they went on to crush the 76'ers by 22 points. Shortly following Kyrie Irving's return the Cavs went on an impressive 8-game winning streak. Things were looking good for them until midway through the season where they began to lose more games. The consistency problem they faced in the finals began to creep up on them again. Despite LeBron playing some of the best basketball of his career, the team began to struggle. The Cavs felt that they needed a change that would put them in a favorable position before they headed into the playoffs. They needed not only a lineup adjustment, but also a management adjustment.

Their starting center Timofey Mozgov was not really working out for them as they had originally planned. He wasn't the kind of defensive and offensive threat they needed from a starting center. They needed someone to make a statement in the post and be aggressive when it really counted. Coach David Blatt decided to start the 6'9 monster Tristan Thompson over Timofey Mozgov. Tristan Thompson had proven that he could score effectively in the paint and be an aggressive defensive force. Before his getting his starting position he was averaging roughly 8 points and 10 rebounds per game. He was a consistent off the bench player and with him at the starting 5 position the Cavs would only see improvement heading towards the end of the season.

In terms of management coach David Blatt was no stranger to winning, but he wasn't the kind of coach that they Cavaliers needed right now. He was a leading force in helping to get the Cavs to the finals. The issue was that him and LeBron never really agreed on how the Cavs needed to play in order to win a championship. Coach Blatt came on to rescue a struggling Cleveland team when LeBron wasn't a part of them and the sudden jump to the NBA finals the first season LeBron came back home was not something he was prepared for. They had mutual respect between each other, but deep down they both knew that it was time for a change.

Shortly after Tristan Thompson was moved to the starting center position, assistant coach Tyron Lue was named the head coach of the Cavs and David Blatt was let go. Tyron Lue was a younger coach with an attitude that the other players enjoyed. With a slight improvement in their starting lineup and a new head coach, the Cavs felt they had made the necessary adjustments to finish the rest of the season strong and get ready for the playoffs. They finished 1st in the NBA Eastern Conference that season with a 57-25 record. That season LeBron averaged 25.3 points, 7.4 rebounds and 6.8 assists per game.

In their first round of playoffs they faced the Detroit Pistons whom they had no trouble beating in a 4 game sweep. LeBron played efficiently in all of those games, taking smart shots and averaging over 50% from the field. Kyrie Irving was also playing extremely well in the first round of playoffs. In the first four games against the Pistons he averaged 27.5 points per game on an impressive 47% shooting from the field. Kevin Love was also playing extremely well, averaging a double-double through the first 4 games and scoring over 18 points per game.

In their second round of playoffs they faced the Atlanta Hawks. LeBron and the Cavs had no problem beating the Hawks in four games. They beat the Hawks by 11 points in Game 1, 25 points in Game 2, 13 points in Game 3 and 1 point in Game 4. They were completely unstoppable and were determined to win the championship this season.

In the Eastern Conference finals the Cavs faced the Toronto Raptors. In Game 1 the Cavs completely dismantled the Raptors and beat them by 31 points. They had now won 9 straight playoffs games and were hungry for their 10th. This was how they needed to play in order to win the championship. In Game 1 LeBron dropped 24 points in just 28 minutes of play. His efficiency in the playoffs was something out of a video game. Kyrie Irving added 27 points to the Cavs victory and Kevin Love contributed 14 points. The Cavs went on to win Game 2 with ease and racked up their 10th consecutive playoff win. It was a performance for the record books. In Games 3 and 4 the Cavs struggled on the defensive end and lost both games. The series were now tied at 2-2 and the Raptors had put a stop to their playoff winning streak. The Cavs quickly realized that they could not allow themselves to lose their momentum as they had done before. In Game 5 the Cavs played an incredible game and absolutely destroyed the Hawks. They beat the Hawks by 38 points and it was one of the biggest playoff blowouts in NBA history. The Game 5 win set the tone for the next game and the Cavs went on to win Game 6 by 26 points and became the 2016 Eastern Conference champions. They were once again back in the finals to face the Warriors who had just set the best new regular-season record with 73 wins and only 9 losses. The Warriors had broken the 1995-96 Chicago Bulls record of 72 wins and 10 losses. There was no denying that the Warriors were an amazing team. One thing was for certain, the finals were going to be an absolute battle.

2015-2016 NBA FINALS

Game 1

Game 1 of the 2015-2016 NBA finals was an away game for the Cavaliers and the Warriors rarely lost home games of this stature. LeBron would have to play at his best if the Cavs were to have any chance of winning. Steph Curry and Klay Thompson both ended playing terrible in Game 1. Steph Curry only scored 11 points and Klay Thompson only had 9, yet the Warriors still somehow managed to win the game. The Warriors bench players Andre Iquodala, Sean Livingston and Leandro Barbosa came in clutch for them in the second half of the game and helped them pull away a lead that the Cavs failed to come back from. They ended up winning the game 104-89 and the Cavs were left stunned at how they let the game slip away after the first half. Despite LeBron's amazing performance of 23 points, 12 rebounds and 9 assists the Cavs lost Game 1 by 15 points. LeBron needed to step up and be the leader that the Cavs needed or they would suffer the same fate as the previous season.

Game 2

It was back at the Oracle Arena for Game 2 and it was time for LeBron to step up and lead his team to victory. Unfortunately, the Warriors had other plans for LeBron and the Cavaliers. In Game 2 the whole Cavs team struggled to find their offensive flow and ended up getting blown out by the Warriors 110-77. They Cavs managed to do the exact same thing as they did in Game 1, they let the game slip away in the second half. The Warriors ended up going on a 20-2 run during the first half and Kevin Love suffered a head injury during that time trying to grab a rebound. Love played the rest of the period, but was out the second half of the game in which Draymond Green was simply unstoppable. Green finished the game with 28 points, 7 rebounds and 5 assists. The Warriors managed to keep LeBron under 20 points and held Kyrie to only 10 points. The Warriors were now up 2-0 in the finals and LeBron had to decide how bad he wanted to bring home a title to Cleveland. He had to step up and be the superstar player that everyone knows he is.

Game 3

With home court advantage in Game 3, it was time for LeBron to show fans and critics why he was the King. In Game 3 it was obvious to everyone that LeBron was playing with pure determination and heart. With Kevin Love out for Game 3 due to his head injury, LeBron knew he needed to look deep within himself to perform, but also rely on his teammates. Old school veteran Richard Jefferson ended up starting for Kevin Love and managed to have a very solid performance. LeBron didn't care that the Cavs were down 2-0, he just wanted to go out there and win the game. The Cavaliers ended up not only beating the Warriors, but beating them badly. The Cavaliers won 120-90 and proved that they still had a fighting chance for the championship. LeBron had 32 points, 11 rebounds and 6 assists. Kyrie Irving dropped 30 points, 4 rebounds and 8 assists. J.R. Smith had 20 points, 4 rebounds and 1 assist. Richard Jefferson had a solid night with 9 points, 8 rebounds and 2 assists. Tristan Thompson ended up having an amazing night with 14 points and 13 boards. The Cavs had proven that they could step up and perform when it mattered.

Game 4

The Quicken Loans Arena was packed full of fans who still believed in LeBron and the Cavs. Game 4 was tight in the first half, but the Warriors managed to pull away from the Cavs in the second half and win 108-97. Steph Curry was absolutely on fire from the field. He dropped 38 points, 6 rebounds and 7 assists. He made an incredible 7 out of 13 three pointers. LeBron had an amazing game with 25 points, 13 rebounds and 9 assists.

He was just one assist away from a triple double, but his stats didn't really matter too much if his team lost the game. Draymond Green was slapped with his fourth flagrant foul of the playoffs which resulted in a Game 5 suspension for him. The Warriors were now up 3-1 in the finals and everyone thought it was over. No team in NBA history has ever come back from a 3-1 deficit in the Finals. LeBron and the Cavs needed a miracle and LeBron wasn't scared to make NBA history.

Game 5

Game 5 was an away game for the Cavaliers and this was it. They had to win the game or they would be sent home packing. It was a very close game going into the second half until the Cavaliers pulled away and managed to win the game 112-97. LeBron James and Kyrie Irving both dropped 41 points and became the first teammates in NBA finals history to score 40 or more points in the same game. James also collected 16 rebounds to help the Cavs win and advance to Game 6. Steph Curry and Klay Thompson both played a great game with Curry dropping 25 points and 7 rebounds while Thompson poured in 37 points along with 3 rebounds. Many people believed that if Draymond Green didn't get suspended for Game 5 that the Cavs would have lost. One thing was for certain, the King wasn't ready to give up yet.

Game 6

Game 6 was back home at the Quicken Loans Arena in Cleveland, Ohio. The Cavs started the game off hot scoring the first 8 points and then outscoring the Warriors by 20 points in the first quarter. The Cavs absolutely destroyed the Warriors in the first quarter 31-11. In the second half, Cleveland continued to dominate the Warriors on the offensive end and managed to win the game 115-101. LeBron went on an absolute scoring rampage and scored 18 straight points for the Cavaliers from the end of the third quarter to the middle of the fourth quarter. He was absolutely relentless and refused to lose. Steph Curry ended up fouling out of the game in the fourth quarter and it was fair to say the LeBron got in his head. Winning Game 6 was a testament to LeBron's dedication to bring home a championship to the city of Cleveland. LeBron played an incredible game consisting of 41 points, 8 rebounds and 11 assists. Tristan Thompson was an absolute beast in Game 6 scoring 15 points and racking up 16 rebounds. Kyrie Irving contributed 23 points, 4 assists and 3 rebounds. LeBron never doubted himself or his teammates. Despite being 3-1 in the finals, LeBron knew that if he stayed focused and determined his team could come back and win the championship. Game 7 would go down in history as one of the most iconic finals games of all time.

Game 7

It was back at the Oracle Arena in Oakland

California for Game 7 and the pressure was on for both teams. Game 7 was one of the closest NBA finals of all time. There were 20 lead changes and 11 instances of the game being tied up. The first quarter was very close with Cleveland leading the Warriors 23-22. Both teams were fighting extremely hard during every single possession and had the fans on their feet every time a basket was made. By half-time the Warriors led the Cavs 49-42. LeBron knew that the Cavs could not allow themselves to crumble as they had done the previous year. As they began the second half, the Cavs looked determined and ready to leave everything on the court. By the end of the third quarter the Cavs managed to outscore the Warriors 33-27 and now the Warriors only had a 1 point lead going into the fourth quarter. The 4 quarter was extremely tight and both teams played with laser accuracy. It was the lowest scoring quarter of the entire series. With 1:50 remaining in the 4th quarter and the game tied up at 89, LeBron delivered one of the most iconic blocks of all time on a breakaway layup by Andre Iguodala. LeBron raced the entire length of the court and managed to pin the ball on the backboard preventing Andre Iquadala from scoring which would have given the Warriors a 2-point lead. A lot of players have the ability to get the crowd loud and excited for the game, but only a few special players like LeBron can silence them. That's exactly what he did with his spectacular block. The Warriors fans were completely quiet after the block and the ball was back in Cleveland's possession. The next possession down LeBron had the ball in his hand and ran down the clock to take a right-hand hook shot inside the paint which ended up missing. The rebound got tipped and the ball ended up in Steph Curry's hands. With 1:25 left to go in the game Steph Curry dribbled the ball down at the top of the key and shot a three-pointer which ended up missing the rim completely and the rebound was picked up by Kevin Love. Kevin Love passed the ball to Kyrie Irving and after Kyrie dribbled passed the half-court line coach Tyronn Lue called for a timeout with 1:09 remaining. With the game still tied at 89 the pressure to make a shot was coming down on both teams. The ball was inbounded to Kyrie with Klay Thompson guarding him tight at the top of the key. JR Smith ended up setting a pick for Kyrie at the top of the key which caused Klay Thompson and Steph Curry to switch. Curry was now guarding Irving who was trying to wind down the clock before taking a final shot. With 55 seconds left to go in the game Kyrie dribbled a few times, gave Curry a small jab crossover and launched a fade away three-pointer that went straight in. After Kyrie made the shot the commentators could barely keep their excitement. ***"ITS GOOD, Kyrie Irving from downtown"****,* yelled one of the commentators as the Cavs made their way back on defense. The Cavs were now up 92-89 and LeBron could almost taste the championship. The next possession down the Cavs had Kevin Love guarding Steph Curry who was going to take the final shot. Kevin Love was all over him and caused him to take an off balance three-pointer which ended up missing. The Warriors and the Cavs both had one foul left to give and on the next run down LeBron ended up getting fouled at the top of the key. LeBron inbounded the ball to Kyrie Irving with 18.7

seconds remaining in the game and 14 seconds remaining on the shot clock. LeBron and the Cavs were now seconds away from winning the championship. Kyrie had the ball in the back court guarded by Klay Thompson. He dribbled the full length of the court and headed towards the rim and quickly dished out the ball the LeBron who was just coming towards the paint. LeBron got the ball and went up for a monster dunk to seal the game away, but ended up missing as he got fouled hard by Draymond Green. There were 10.6 seconds remaining in the game with LeBron heading to the line to shoot two free-throws. With the Warriors fans chanting loudly LeBron took his first free-throw and ended up missing. LeBron lined up to take his second free-throw and this was his chance to put the game away for good. With his heart racing, sweat dripping down his face, and the city of Cleveland on his back he took the final free throw and sunk it. The Cavs were now up 93-89 and the Warriors would need a miracle in order to win. The Warriors would not be able to score again. As the final buzzer went off, the entire Cleveland

Cavaliers bench rushed to the floor. As his teammates were hugging and congratulating LeBron he got down on his knees and was overcome with joy and emotion. LeBron had delivered on his promise to come home and bring a championship to his beloved hometown. LeBron finished the game with a triple double consisting of 27 points, 11 rebounds and 11 assists. The Cavaliers made NBA history as the first team to ever come back from a 3-1 deficit to win an NBA title. LeBron was named the NBA finals MVP for the third time in his career and became the fifth player to ever win the award three times. Cleveland's long years of basketball nightmares had finally ended after going 52 years without winning a championship. LeBron could not have pulled it off without the help of a team and organization that believed in him and his god given talents. After playing 13 years in the league, LeBron had finally done it. The kid from Akron brought home a championship to the city of Cleveland. The next big was question was would LeBron be able to surpass the great Michael Jordan? Would he live to be remembered as the greatest basketball player of all time? We will one day find out.

Chapter 7: The Stats Season By Season

Season	Age	Tm	FG%	3P%	FT%	TRB	AST	STL	BLK	PTS
2003-04	19	CLE	42%	29%	75%	5.5	5.9	1.6	0.7	20.9
2004-05	20	CLE	47%	35%	75%	7.4	7.2	2.2	0.7	27.2
2005-06	21	CLE	48%	34%	74%	7	6.6	1.6	0.8	31.4
2006-07	22	CLE	48%	32%	70%	6.7	6	1.6	0.7	27.3
2007-08	23	CLE	48%	32%	71%	7.9	7.2	1.8	1.1	30
2008-09	24	CLE	49%	34%	78%	7.6	7.2	1.7	1.1	28.4
2009-10	25	CLE	50%	33%	77%	7.3	8.6	1.6	1	29.7
2010-11	26	MIA	51%	33%	76%	7.5	7	1.6	0.6	26.7
2011-12	27	MIA	53%	36%	77%	7.9	6.2	1.9	0.8	27.1
2012-13	28	MIA	57%	41%	75%	8	7.3	1.7	0.9	26.8
2013-14	29	MIA	57%	38%	75%	6.9	6.3	1.6	0.3	27.1
2014-15	30	CLE	49%	35%	71%	6	7.4	1.6	0.7	25.3
2015-16	31	CLE	52%	31%	73%	7.4	6.8	1.4	0.6	25.3

CH8. ENDORSEMENTS & EARNINGS

ENDORSEMENT DEALS (ESTIMATED)

Lebron's Estimated Endorsement Deals		
Company	Year	Estimated Amount
Nike	2003-2010	$90,000,000
Upper Deck	2003-2004	$5,000,000
Coca Cola	2003-2008	$10,000,000
Bubblicious	2004-2008	$5,000,000
Juice Batteries	2004-2008	$8,000,000
Upper Deck	2004-2010	$6,000,000
State Farm	2006-2007	$4,000,000
Microsoft	2007-2008	$2,000,000
Cub Cadet	2008-2009	$1,000,000
Coca Cola	2008-2015	$16,000,000
McDonald's	2010-2015	$15,000,000
Nike	2010-2015	$50,000,000
Samsung	2011-2015	$8,000,000
Dunkin' Donuts	2012-2015	$20,000,000
Tencent	2013-2015	$15,000,000
Audemars Piguet	2013-2014	$2,000,000
Kia	2014-2015	$10,000,000

Chapter 9: Off The Court

Many people know LeBron for his incredible basketball talents, but others know him for his incredible work off the court. Off the court LeBron works with the community whenever he can. In 2004, LeBron and his mother established the LeBron James Family Foundation. They established the organization in order to help out children and single-parent families in need. There are many different programs within the organization, but the overall mission is to leave a positive effect on the lives of children and young adults. The organization accomplishes this through education and extra-curricular activities and initiatives. The foundation focuses on the following initiatives.

- Wheels For Education
- Akron I Promise Network
- The LeBron Advisory Board
- St. Vincent – St. Mary High School
- University of Akron Ohio
- Boys and Girls Club

Each foundation has a slightly different goal, but each strives to make a difference in the lives of those less fortunate.

The **Wheels For Education** program began in 2011 when James partnered up with State Farm to create a campaign which focused on the issue of national dropout. Wheels for Education provides support to third graders in Akron public schools to make sure they make it to graduation. A recent survey done by the Akron public school district showed that roughly 91% of parents with kids who participated in the Wheels for Education program performed better academically. This is a great accomplishment for LeBron's foundation, but there is more.

In 2015, LeBron made the public announcement that he would be giving children the opportunity to attend college for free. In order to fully put his plan to action, LeBron teamed up with the University of Akron to make it happen. The University of Akron would give full ride scholarships to over 1,100 kids who participate in LeBron's **I Promise program**. The eligibility for kids to participate in the program ranges from third to seventh grade. The rules stipulate that if they complete the program and meet all the requirements, their tuition costs would be covered by LeBron's foundation and the University of Akron beginning in 2021. This is a huge commitment of over $41 million dollars by LeBron and it goes to show just what kind of leader and selfless individual he is.

LeBron's generosity doesn't end there. His foundation is also donating over $1 million for a full renovation of the St. Vincent – St. Mary high school gym where LeBron once played. This will include new sports equipment, locker rooms, uniforms and so much more. Giving back to his school where he once played says a lot about the character and dedication of LeBron to improve his hometown.

On top of his own foundation LeBron is highly involved with the **Boy's and Girl's Club**. In 2010 he helped raise over $2.5 million for the club. In 2015 he helped to renovate the Boys and Girls club in Manhattan, New York. Aside from being one of the best basketball players of all time, he is also considered to be one of the most charitable athletes of his generation. His relentless drive, talent, perseverance and hard work on and off the court, define him as a true champion.

About the Author

I hope you have enjoyed reading the amazing journey of one of the best basketball players to ever play the game. It gives me pleasure and joy to give people the story behind one of the greatest athletes of all time. If you have enjoyed reading this book I have done my job as this is my true passion. Please be on the lookout for my next title about one of the most dynamic point guards in NBA history, Allen Iverson. I look forward to seeing you again.

Printed in Poland
by Amazon Fulfillment
Poland Sp. z o.o., Wrocław